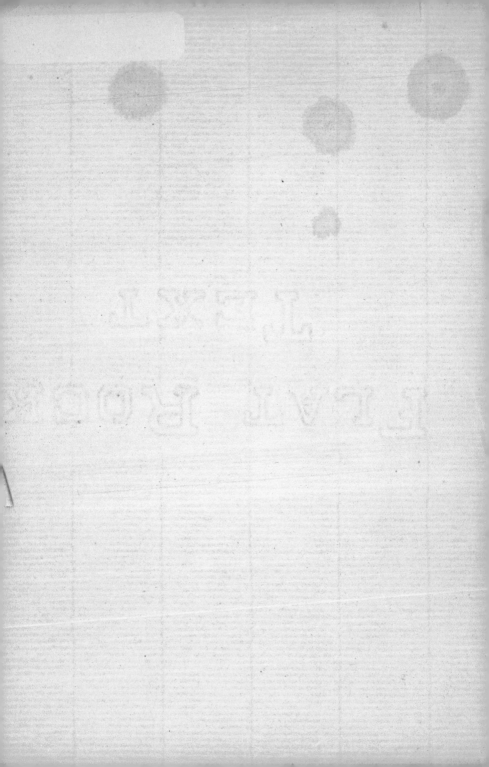

AUTOBIOGRAPHY

OF

A FARM BOY

BY

ISAAC PHILLIPS ROBERTS, M. Agr.

Professor Emeritus and for thirty years Professor
and Dean of the College of Agriculture
Cornell University

ALBANY
J. B. LYON COMPANY, PUBLISHERS
1916

PORTRAIT OF PROFESSOR ROBERTS

Painted in 1903 by Collins and now in Roberts Hall, Cornell University.

CONTENTS

STATEMENT BY L. H. BAILEY

For thirty years Professor Roberts led the work in agriculture at Cornell University. These were the eventful and triumphant years of 1873 to 1903. They began in doubt and with small things, but they were large with faith. He developed one of the best institutions of its kind.

Only ten or eleven years had elapsed since the passage of the Land Grant Act, at which time instruction in agriculture was given a national sanction. A few colleges had made the effort to organize the subject into teaching form and to collect the equipment and develop the farms that were necessary to the new enterprise. Even Michigan, the oldest of the existing North American colleges of agriculture, had been under way only sixteen years. Cornell had given instruction five years. From the first, agriculture had had its appointed place in the institution; but the work was not really established until Professor Roberts came. He came from a farm and with the traditions of farming. He had had experience in the new institution in Iowa. He put himself to the task bravely, as one sets out to plow and to fit a prairie domain the boundaries of which are unseen and the promise of which is unknown but to the few.

For thirty years Professor Roberts and his associates stood for agriculture, always for agriculture — not for natural science under the name of agriculture nor for some pleasant combination of studies that would satisfy the law. In an eastern university, with the great tide of emigration sweeping past him to the West, with decreasing values, with old fields, with hindering traditions, he stood,— stood like a prophet.

It is this courage, this steadfastness in the determination to hold the field for agriculture, that grows larger in my estimation as the years go by. I speak of his work in the past tense, for I too look backward; but I am glad that he is still keen to follow the result of his labors. It was not then a day for erudition, or for high technical scholarship, but a time for clear faith, homely and direct relations with the people, wisdom in giving advice. From the first years that I knew him he was a philosopher and a forecaster, always practical, always driving home the point, always with his feet squarely on the ground.

He loved the farm; from the rail fence to the back lot, the trees in the pasture, the woodside, the orchard, every animal in stall or field, the high land and the low land, all were his to walk over, to question, to inspect with care, and to improve. It was one of the delights of his teaching to take his " boys " to the farm. He was a master in the practice of observing farm conditions,— why the grass was thin here and heavy there, why the weeds came in, why the animals chose the spot on which to lie, how to run the drains, to build a fence, to put up a shed or barn, to paint a building, how to break a horse, how to breed a herd from a common foundation, how to sell a crop, what the weather meant, how to bring an old field back into good condition. He did not teach some small department of farm knowledge as we do in these days, but the whole farm and the farmer and the wife and the children and the hired man; and he taught it with a quiet and genial philosophy, often quaint and always full of good humor. He was the real teacher of the small group, preferring the out-of-doors and the barns and the herds to the formal laboratories. I have never known anyone to make such good educational use of an entire farm and its equipment.

Yet, with all his knowledge of the fields, Professor Roberts was singularly sympathetic with every range of science teaching, with every indoor laboratory, with good work in every department of knowledge. Unlike many practical men, he did not insist that all science should have immediate application. He saw the educational result. So he gathered about him many specialists, gave them every facility and equipment he could secure, and left them with great freedom.

His hold on the students and on the people of the state was remarkable. His talks and addresses always had practical wisdom combined with vision, he was patient and self-contained under criticism, he made friends and he held them. To this day all over New York his students hold him in affection, and old men with broken step inquire of him with tenderness.

Professor Roberts retired at seventy, but fortunately retained his connection with Cornell as professor emeritus, a relationship that he still holds. The men of his active generation have mostly passed the years of service. Many of his immediately succeeding colleagues carry still the responsibilities that he left to them, and they are ever mindful of what he would have them to do.

OUTLINE OF
PROFESSOR ROBERTS' LIFE

THE author of this autobiography, Professor Isaac Phillips Roberts, was born in Seneca County, New York, July 24, 1833, of native American parents. His father, Aaron Phillips Roberts, emigrated from Harbortown, New Jersey, to Central New York about 1816 and in 1820 married Elizabeth Burroughs, the daughter of Joseph Burroughs, who had come from the same neighborhood in New Jersey in 1812. Professor Roberts was educated in the district school of the town of Varick and at the Seneca Falls Academy. He never attended College but in 1875 he received from the Iowa State Agricultural College the degree of Master of Agriculture.

In early manhood he went from East Varick to La Porte, Indiana, where he practised the trade of carpenter until he was able to buy a farm, and taught school during the winters. In 1857 he married at Kingsbury, Indiana, Margaret Jane Marr, the daughter of a prosperous farmer, and in 1862 emigrated with his wife and daughter in a pioneer wagon from Indiana to Mount Pleasant, Iowa, where he settled down to farming.

In 1869 he was called to the position of Superintendent of the Farm and Secretary of the Board of Trustees of the Iowa Agricultural College at Ames, and shortly afterward was made Professor of Agriculture. In 1873 he accepted a similar position at Cornell University, Ithaca, New York, and a little later was made Dean of the Faculty of Agriculture and Director of the Experiment Station. During the thirty years of his service at Cornell he wrote voluminously on agricultural subjects, as Associate Editor on the staff of *The Country Gentleman,* about fourteen hundred short articles chiefly in answer to queries; and four scientific books, i. e., *The Fertility of The Land* which has gone to several editions and is still in general use as a College textbook; *The Farmers' Business Handbook* of which a second edition has recently been published; *The Farmstead* and *The Horse.*

At the age of seventy he retired with the title of Professor Emeritus, receiving an honorary pension from the Carnegie Foundation for his services; and settled in Palo Alto, California. At the death of his wife in December, 1913, he went to live with his youngest son at Fresno, California, where he spends his winters. In the summer of 1915 he finished this narrative at the home of his daughter in Berkeley, California.

HOW I CAME
TO WRITE THIS BOOK

WHEN my sons and daughter were little they, like other children, wanted me to tell them stories; and as I had never read much fiction and was not very imaginative, I used to describe how things were made and relate the simple adventures of my limited travels. But best of all they liked the stories of my boyhood and the tales of the neighborhood in which I was born and grew to manhood. The country of my nativity — East Varick, Seneca County, New York — is situated on the west bank of Cayuga Lake, about opposite the town of Aurora, and when they went there later to visit their relatives it appeared to be an old settled place. But to me it always had the glamour of a pioneer region, for it was a wilderness when my grandparents came from New Jersey to settle there in 1812, and the tales of their experiences and of my parents' early life had all the picturesqueness of western adventure.

Since I retired from my professorship at Cornell University in 1903 and moved to California, my children have repeatedly asked me to write out in detail not only those early recollections but a complete autobiography. My daughter, Mary, on one of her visits to the old homestead of the Roberts family in New York, found some tattered yellow papers in a market basket under the business desk belonging to my eldest brother, Ralph. These proved to be the private papers of her great-grandfather, Joseph Burroughs, which had been taken from an old desk in the Burroughs farmhouse and which would have been destroyed, perhaps, but for her interest in them.

These documents — essays, poems, riddles, *et cetera,*— had no great literary merit but reflected the taste of the time and showed that my grandfather Burroughs, who was a school teacher in his youth and a farmer throughout his adult life, had, at any rate, intellectual aspirations. My daughter, therefore, proposed that I should continue the literary tradition and leave this informal account of my life to my children and grandchildren.

I realize that this is a somewhat difficult undertaking, as I have no notes or letters of the earlier period to guide me, the few papers I had having been destroyed when my house was burned in 1863. In old age, however, one is likely to remember the scenes of youth better than those of later years; though one is apt also to exaggerate the importance of happenings in youth and to get some things out of focus. As to dates, many of them will not be exact, and I shall often have to say " about "; but, at any rate, I shall not set down anything in malice nor for the purpose of leading my children and friends to think " What a big man am I ".

I began this autobiography in 1904-5 and handed over a lengthy manuscript to my daughter for criticism. But on April 18, 1906, at 5.20 in the morning, a severe earthquake occurred in San Francisco, California, where she was then living. Fires soon afterward broke out and, as the water mains were shattered, the flames spread almost immediately and very rapidly. Mary was living at a Settlement on South Park near Third Street at that time and lost nearly all of her belongings, my manuscript with the rest.

In Palo Alto, where I was living, the chimney of our house was destroyed, as were almost all the others in the town; much plastering cracked and fell, a few buildings were thrown out of plumb and two recently constructed concrete-block buildings were leveled to the ground. The Stanford University buildings suffered most, the damage to them being estimated at more than one-half million dollars. The greatest movement or cleavage was along the foothills near which the University buildings stand; and in one place the slip of the earth was at least six feet, as shown by the board fences. But it is not my purpose to give a detailed account of the earthquake and fire, as that can be found elsewhere, in print — only to relate so much of it as came within my purview.

One more digression I must permit myself before I set out on my personal narrative. If this history of a farm boy should ever come to print, I should not expect that it would interest the literary men of that time, but I should hope that it might give courage to boys on the farms who are often denied opportunity to acquire a thorough education by reason of lack of means and too strenuous physical labor. Theodore Roosevelt has said that he began to get his education young — right away after he left college. It will be seen that I began mine at a much earlier date and continued it for three-quarters of a century. The farm boys who may read this should learn from it the lesson of *continuous* growth, by which even the slowest may arrive at their full capacity.

SECTION I

BOYHOOD AND YOUTH IN NEW YORK STATE

(1833-1854)

SECTION I

BOYHOOD AND YOUTH IN NEW YORK STATE

I WAS born in the Roberts' farmhouse, on the west bank of Cayuga Lake, July 24, 1833, at sunrise of a fine harvest morning. At that time and for several years subsequently it was the custom of my father — as of other heads of families — to go to the nearest village, Seneca Falls, some days in advance of harvest and there to trade farm products and to purchase supplies enough to last for as much as six weeks, that is, through harvest. There was always on hand an abundance of pickled pork — the great, de-ribbed sides of the hogs killed the fall before, which had been packed edgewise in concentric layers in huge casks and left in the cellar covered with saturated brine to which a little salt petre had been added. But groceries, such as sugar, molasses, spices and a keg of salt mackerel to break the monotony of pork and chicken, were purchased in town; and most important of all items was the keg of whiskey, for few men would work in those days without a regular supply of some kind of spirituous liquors.   Although we had an overment of home-grown foods, I have mentioned these purchases to leave on record the fact that the New York pioneers were most bountifully fed — a great factor in the upbuilding of a vigorous people.

As to the desirability of whiskey as a beverage, my earliest experience as well as my later ones lead me to an unfavorable opinion; for, on the morning I was born, the hired woman helped herself to the whiskey and before breakfast time she was unable to perform her duties.   This left all the housework for a family consisting of an invalid mother, five children and some half dozen harvest hands, to be done by my eldest sister Caroline (who was only twelve years of age), with such assistance as the other children could render.

I imagine, therefore, that I was an inopportune if not an unwelcome visitor, especially as I came for a long stay, with no idea of entertaining myself.   But, in spite of such a beginning, I have thought myself fortunate in being nearly the middle child of parents who were themselves middle children; and I am sure that I was fortunate in being born in the great Empire State and in its most fertile and beautiful section, by the shores of one of its clear and lovely "finger" lakes. For I cannot but think that "Old Cayuga" had a profound if unconscious influence in preparing me for an unusually strenuous and difficult life.

The house where I was born was on the site of the log house built by my grandfather Burroughs when he emigrated from Harbortown, New Jersey, to Central New York, in 1812. At that time he brought with him his family, consisting of a wife and three children, traveling in a prairie-schooner wagon. He had selected a farm there some time before, I think, and had built this log house — at any rate, there was a house upon the site when they arrived. A few miles before they reached their place he stopped at a saw-mill and bought a single, wide board which served as their first dining table. This was constructed by boring holes into the logs of the house, and driving pins into them that supported the board. The larger part of the furniture was home-made. Every farmer in those days was provided with a small kit of rough carpenter tools and was trained after the manner of the skilled Dutchman of Pennsylvania who claimed that if he had a broad-ax and a narrow ax, an auger, a saw, a pair of compasses and a two-foot rule, he could build a saw-mill.

As is customary among farmers in a new country, a barn was built before the second or permanent dwelling house.　Just when my grandfather built the permanent residence I cannot say,
but it must have been fully ninety years ago; and
it must have been a well-built house, for it is still
in good condition.　The construction was somewhat peculiar as compared with present methods.
About every three feet along the outer walls of
the house, hewn posts which were at least eight
by eight inches, were erected and held together
about five feet from their tops by great beams
upon which the upper floor was laid.　The beams
having been planed and the boards also, on both
sides, it was not by any means an inartistic structure, seen from the inside.　The space — eight to
ten inches — between the inner plastered walls and
the outside clap-boarded ones, was filled with clay
mortar held in place by thin strips of wood which
had been split out of straight grained logs.

The pioneers had a unique way of mixing mortar: they excavated the surface soil, dug up the
clay beneath, then threw in straw, and some corn,
poured water over all, and turned in a herd of hungry swine to do the work of mixing.　The eave-
troughs of this house were made of a stick of

cucumber timber about six by eight inches, hollowed out on the inside and moulded on the outside, and these, when spiked under the eaves, not only served to convey water but formed a very respectable cornice as well. They did efficient service for more than thirty years. At the time I was born there was also a barn, a long cow stable, a wagon-house, a wood-house, a stone ash-house, a smoke-house and an out-door brick oven.

The Family

Such knowledge as I have of my forebears on both sides indicates that they were farmers, almost without exception and chiefly of Welsh and English extraction. Some of them fought in the Revolution but, so far as I know, without particular distinction. My maternal grandfather, Joseph Burroughs, was born in Hunterdon County, New Jersey, probably about 1769. He appears to have begun life as a school teacher, for a certificate of his superior qualifications exists in the Roberts family Bible, owned by Ralph P. Roberts of East Varick, New York. The certificate is signed by twelve Dutch school trustees. It is known that the Burroughs family emigrated from New Jersey to Central New York in 1812 and settled in Seneca

County, on the west bank of Cayuga Lake, at the place now called East Varick.

As I have already mentioned, Grandfather Burroughs was a voluminous writer, for each of my children now possesses a number of his manuscripts which were recovered some forty years after his death. The handwriting is good, the grammar nearly faultless and the subjects cover a wide range. He must certainly have had an active mind and literary tastes to find time to write so profusely while he was farming and letting sunlight into beech and maple forests which were then so dense that they would yield from twenty to twenty-five cords of four-foot wood per acre.

It appears from the internal evidence of these papers that Joseph Burroughs was a farmer, a local poet and speaker, accustomed to commemorate the notable events of the neighborhood and to have these productions published in the Ovid *Gazette*. He was a tax assessor and a school trustee; a member of the Methodist Church though rather too liberal in his opinions to please the minister; a man widely interested in national affairs, as shown by the varied subjects of his writings; violently opposed to the Free Masons; and if not well educated, at least well read in classical English literature, for his verse abounds in classical

allusions after the fashion of the period. Pope
and Dryden appear to have been his literary
models; and that he was full of sentiment is indi-
cated by the great variety of elegiac and love
poetry as well as of satire, left to us. He evidently
delighted in puzzles, enigmas and difficult arith-
metical problems.

I know very little about my grandparents on my
father's side because they did not emigrate to New
York but lived and died in the neighborhood of
Hunterdon County, New Jersey. My father,
Aaron Phillips Roberts, was born there, October
24, 1795, near Harbortown, which is not far from
Washington's Crossing on the Delaware River.
When he was about twenty-one years of age he
walked from Harbortown to East Varick — a
distance of three hundred miles — with his gun on
his shoulder. When he married my mother, Elizabeth Burroughs, in 1820, the young couple went to
live in a log cabin on a small farm of about thirty-
five acres, upon which tract the village of East
Varick now stands. After Grandfather Burroughs' death they moved back to the old homestead farm and worked the two farms together
until their eldest daughter, Caroline, married
Charles Christopher, when the East Varick tract
was given to her.

My father, in early life, I have been told, taught
school one winter and singing school for several
winters, using the " buckwheat " note-book. When
he was about forty years of age he ceased to work
regularly on the farm with the hired men and contented himself with cultivating an excellent garden,
cutting up some of the wood after it had been
hauled to the house, and in winter with feeding a
portion of the livestock; he generally worked mod-
erately in harvest and haying time. He was a
great reader and kept himself well informed on
the happenings of the day, but he talked little and
was rather reserved toward the neighboring farmers. The picture of him that rises in my mind is
of a dignified country squire in his high, light-
colored hat stored with letters and papers, high
boots and a " shad-belly " coat. I never knew him
to wear either overalls or a blouse when at work —
these might be suitable for the hired men and the
boys, but not for the landowner. It will be seen
that he still kept some of the dignity and exclu-
siveness of the old country gentleman and landowner of England.

My mother, Elizabeth Burroughs, was also born
near Harbortown, New Jersey, August 16, 1800,
and came to East Varick with her parents when
they settled there in 1812. It was she who stood

at the center of the household. It was she who made it possible for me to go forth strong in body and of purpose, to work patiently and bravely for the farmers — for science, for justice and for truth. As I look upon the picture of her strong, rugged, placid face, I recall her self-sacrificing life for the good of everyone within the sphere of her influence; and I know that she was a Christian, although she belonged to no church and seldom attended one.

Soon after marriage at twenty years of age, her toils began, and as the years passed, griefs and burdens followed on one another's trail; but she bore them all quietly, lovingly, even smilingly. I see her now, the central figure in that numerous, growing family — commanding, handsome, but not beautiful, with that large benignity which comes to middle-life and age, from a well-spent, unselfish life. From the youngest to the oldest child, we all looked to her for comfort in trouble, for instruction and advice in all our undertakings, and for appreciation in our successes. After all these years I cannot forgive myself for having wantonly disobeyed her when she forbade me to attend a dance at a tavern of doubtful reputation. This was the more inexcusable since I was allowed to do almost anything that was not positively bad.

Such education as she had she received in the
schools of Harbortown, but she never went to
school after she was twelve years of age. She
was, however, a great reader — considering her
cares and opportunities — had a remarkable memory and was clever at mathematics. She could
figure a problem " in her head " more quickly and
accurately than any of her sons. She was particularly fond of *Rasselas,* Aesop's *Fables in Rhyme,*
Thompson's *Seasons* and Scott's *Lady of the Lake,*
the greater part of which she was still able to
quote in her old age. She could not sing at all
nor could any of her generation of the Burroughs
family; but she had an unusual love of poetry and
occasionally wrote letters in verse to her children.

My mother died at the ripe age of seventy-nine
years in the house where she had lived for more
than fifty years and in the midst of loving children
and grandchildren. She had been " Aunt Betsy "
to the whole neighborhood and a friend to everyone who needed anything she could give or could
do for them.

My father and mother were married in 1820, as
I have already said, and the ceremony was performed by the Reverend Palmer Roberts, an uncle
and an itinerant minister of the Methodist Church,

who was a well-known and eccentric person. The story is told of him that once when he was preaching " fire and brimstone " he made a rather pointed personal application to an unregenerate tough in the audience. Some days later the two men met in the roadway, and the man of the pew declared he had been insulted and offered to fight. The minister replied that what he said was true and resorted to argument, but the sinner insisted that he was going to thrash him. The Reverend Roberts got down from his horse, took off his coat, saying: " Lay there, shadbelly, while I lick this sinner!" When he had finished the job he put on his coat and rode away singing:

"Oh how happy are they who their Savior obey
And have laid up their treasure above!"

PIONEER SETTLERS IN SENECA COUNTY

My parents had nine children, of whom only one beside myself — William H. B. Roberts — is now living; and lived during the whole of their married life in the township of East Varick — my mother lived more than fifty years in the house which I have described and which still remains. This township of East Varick, which was about eight miles long, extending from Cayuga Lake to

Seneca Lake, was settled almost altogether by emigrants from New Jersey, of English, Welsh and Irish extraction; while the next township, Fayette, to the north of us, was filled up with Pennsylvania Dutch people. New Jersey was sandy and at that time not very desirable for farming purposes, and as soon as this lake country became known they flocked westward to it. At the time the Burroughs family left New Jersey the farmers there could no longer raise wheat, and they therefore ate rye bread almost exclusively. In those days wheat could be grown only on new land; yet by 1849, those same Jersey lands had been brought back into wheat by the use of lime and clover.

It should be noted in passing that the township, Fayette, whose population was largely "low Dutch," laid less stress upon education and religion than the settlers of Varick; but they were better farmers. They built the first great red "bank" — overshot — barns and kept large, fat, short-legged horses from which arose our expression: "Like a Dutch horse, largest when lying down." In the first generation the Dutch built large wooden, brick or stone houses, and the women worked hard in the open fields, especially at harvest time. But later, when the piano or organ, and the light top-buggy came in, the girls ceased to work in the fields. Some of these people bore what seemed to us American boys very odd names: Libarger, Poffenbarger, Laudenslaker and Kooney. This last was a strange tribe, nicknamed in the countryside as Black Jake, Slivery Jake, Drunken Jake, Jake's Jake and Bully Jake.

As the picture of that lush pioneer life comes back to me I am irresistibly led to philosophize and to compare the earlier with the present time. Then every one was interested in everything that was transpiring and everyone lent a helping hand in all activities. If there were many boys in the family they learned to knit and even to sew, to cook and wash dishes and even to wash soiled clothes. If there were many girls they did the milking, carried in the wood and water, picked the small fruits and gathered the vegetables. It was a co-operative, whole-hearted life, each for all and all for each. In the reading and study hours at night there was the same good-natured comradeship whether in cracking nuts or jokes, in extracting cube root or reading what Horace Greeley knew about farming.

All that they had the members of the family divided and shared. There were no really poor save now and then an unfortunate, worthy poor person, and such were cared for from the common store. The cast-off clothing was not handed out to the mendicant poor but made into rag carpet or deftly converted into patchwork quilts. When a sister was to be married all joined in making useful things for her housekeeping. John was as solicitous for the welfare of the colt which would be his elder brother's when he reached his majority as he was of what he called his own.

In such an atmosphere of mutual helpfulness grew up the people who were later to subdue the wild and windy prairies, to bridge the western rivers and to bind the land together with bands of tempered steel. Not content with reclaiming the prairies, their children moved on to the desert, and beyond into the mountains and foothills, and there spied out the treasure kept for those who had the pluck to find and bring it forth. The more I think of it the more I am persuaded that these pioneers were Christians or near Christians, for of everything they had they divided, in a measure, and a part of it they passed along.

INDUSTRIAL AND SOCIAL CONDITIONS IN MY BOYHOOD

I did not take part in all that I am about to relate in the next paragraphs, but I can assure the reader that I well remember the stories told when I was a lad by my parents as we gathered around the great fire of logs in the living room on winter evenings. In my boyhood the men in harvest time worked from " sun to sun "; if there chanced to be a field of hay or grain nearby they worked for an hour before breakfast and, on rare occasions, harvesting was carried on by moonlight. They had to have an " eye-opener " when they arose and another drink just before sitting down to breakfast. The bottle was carried to the field and two or three drinks apiece were taken during the forenoon by the grown men and one after washing up before dinner, which was served punctually at half-past eleven; but no drink was served after supper.

In harvest time, beside the three regular meals of the day, lunch was served at ten o'clock in the field and again at four if the fields were too distant for the men to come to the house for the five o'clock supper. It may seem that the eating and drinking was excessive, but so was the work. On our farm, hasty beer was provided for the boys and for those who did not care for the stronger drink, and a most acceptable drink it was. The farmers had learned that when only water was drunk, the stomach was in part paralyzed by the large quantities taken to replace the excessive loss of moisture due to the terrible work. This hasty beer was made as follows: a pail of water from the "northeast" corner of the well, a half gill of cider vinegar, one gill of best New Orleans molasses and one to two tablespoons of ginger — stirred thoroughly and modified to suit the taste.

Nearly every farmhouse was provided with a tin horn from four to six feet long, and there was always a rivalry to see who could blow the horn earliest, best and longest. I have known our Pennsylvania hired girl to wind that mammoth horn for fifteen minutes at a stretch. It was in reality a challenge to all farm girls within hearing and, as the farms were small and the horn could be heard for more than a mile with favorable wind, and as the fields were filled with harvesters, she had no mean audience.

I have before me several pages of an old account book of the year 1818 which was kept by my brother Ralph's wife's father, Mr. Grove, who at one time kept a general merchandise store at Sheldrake Point on Cayuga Lake, twelve miles south of our farm. In view of the present agitation concerning the cost of living, the prices quoted are interesting.

ARTICLES	Total Cost in English money			Cost in American money per gal., lb., etc.
	£	s	d	
50 lbs. nails.........	4	3	4	$0.41 per lb.
15 lbs. of 10-oz. cheese.	..	15	8	.25 " "
One padlock.........	..	4	..	1.00
2 bbls. pork.........	16	16	..	42.00 " bbl.
1 gal. rum.........	..	13	6	3.37 " gal.
1 gal. whiskey.......	..	9	..	2.25 " "
2 bu. 45-lbs. wheat..	1	13	..	3.00 " bu.
2 lbs. tobacco	..	6	..	.75 " lb.
1 gal. wine.........	..	16	..	4.00 " gal.
1 lb. tobacco........	..	3	..	.75 " lb.
½ lb. tea............	..	6	..	3.00 " lb.
2 pie dishes.........	..	2	6	.31 " dish.
42½ lbs. of iron......	1	15	5	.22 " lb.
2 hats.............	1	4	..	3.00 each.
1 lb. rasins.........	..	2	..	.50 per lb.
1 bible.............	..	8	..	2.00
½ gal. rum.........	..	5	3	2.62 " gal.
383 ft. boards.......	1	11	..	20.00 " M.
9¾ lbs. steel........	1	4	4	.62 " lb.
1 ft. spinning wheel...	1	16	..	9.00
28 yds. calico........	3	19	4	.71 " yd.
8 lbs. loaf sugar......	1	8	..	.87 " lb.
2 lbs. of shot........	..	3	..	.37 " lb.
½ lb. tea............	..	8	..	4.00 " lb.
7½ lbs. fish..........	..	6	3	.20 " lb.

The English money has been roughly translated into American on the scale of five dollars for a pound, twenty-five cents for a shilling and two cents for a penny. Incidentally I may remark that the English shilling and other small pieces remained in circulation long after the fractional American currency came into use. The following charges probably belong also to the year 1818, although the page is not dated.

1 spade.................	14	..	$3.50
1 barlow knife...........	1	6	.37
5 yds. muslin............	12	6	.62 per yd.
1 scythe................	12	..	3.00
1 gal. whisky...........	9	..	2.25
¼ lb. pepper.............	1	..	1.00 " lb.
½ lb. tea................	6	..	3.00 " lb.

On the page from which the above was taken there are 38 entries, of which 8 are for whiskey; on the next there are 36 charges, of which 8 are for whiskey, gin and rum, 4 for tea, and 2 for tobacco. Page 78 contains a charge for Latinett at $1.44 per yard, and a charge of $7.45 for a bonnet and ribbon, but in all there are 33 items, of which 7 are for spirituous liquors.

I do not remember hearing talk of the high cost of living, although tea was from three to four dollars a pound; nor complaint of the cost of living " low " with wine at four dollars, rum at two to three dollars, and straight whiskey at two twenty-five per gallon. In my boyhood we had always some imported loaf sugar in the house, but it was never used except for company. Ordinarily we used a dark, strong-tasting New Orleans molasses, and occasionally home-made maple sugar for sweetening tea and coffee.

At this time, 1818, there were few orchards in bearing, but I have been told that between 1830 and 1840 my father sold many wagon boxes full of peaches at 6¼ cents per bushel, the purchaser shaking the fruit from the tree and hauling it away to be used in making peach brandy. The sale of fish at the store comes as a surprise, since the lake and the streams were filled with fresh fish merely waiting for some one to drop them a line; but then, as in later years, salted mackerel and white fish were a welcome change from ham and pork in warm weather.

There is one charge of salt in this old account book, but unfortunately the price is not given; but I remember that in those days salt was an expensive luxury, almost as necessary as whiskey and brandy. When a lad I heard the following story which illustrates how difficult it was to procure salt in those days. It was told that on our farm, which was bountifully covered with hard wood, when the land was cleared large trees were cut into lengths some twelve feet long, piled in great heaps, and burned; then the wood ashes were gathered up, leeched, and the lye boiled down in order to secure crude potash salts. My Grandfather Burroughs then loaded the crude product into a skiff which he rowed fifty miles to Syracuse, where it was exchanged for common salt. So precious was this salt that the sacks which contained it were put to soak in a tub, the water afterwards to be boiled down to recover the little that might otherwise have been wasted. Unfortunately, during the night, a horse strayed into the yard and, being salt-hungry, drank too much out of the tub and died. That salt, at any rate, cost more per pound than loaf sugar, one of the seldom used luxuries of the time, for horses were very valuable in those days, oxen being used in place of them even to carry the family to church.

Before the erection of the grist-mill at Seneca Falls, corn, wheat, rye and buckwheat were ground at a little water-mill on the opposite side of the lake and not far from Ithaca. Usually, two sacks nearly filled with "grist" were divided each in the middle, one placed in front and the other at the rear of the saddle and were thus transported on horseback about twelve miles up the Lake following the bridle path; then the grist was loaded into a skiff and carried diagonally across the Lake to the mill. In those days it was a sun-to-sun job with a great part of the night thrown in to get a grist to and from the mill. In 1874, I saw that overshot wheel still intact, although the mill itself — and the water too, in summer — were gone. It was said that the settlers for twenty miles around had been required to raise the frame of the mill at Seneca Falls because of the enormous size of the timbers of which it was constructed.

There are a few personal incidents of my boyhood that remain peculiarly vivid in my memory. The first is a recollection of myself as a small boy, hiding under the currant bushes, but I cannot fix the exact date of that long-to-be-remembered occasion. It happened in this wise: my father was gathering the winter's supply of beets from the garden and piling them near the wood-pile adjoining the lane, so that the tops could be fed to the cows as they came up from the pasture. I undertook to cut off the tops of the beets with an ordinary chopping ax while my younger sister held them on the chopping block for me. Although forbidden to do so I continued and soon chopped off the index finger of my sister's right hand. When I was later discovered under the currant bushes I stoutly declared that my sister had asked me to cut off the tops. In later years I have often meditated on this scene — in our little garden of Eden — for it has been enacted in the world untold times and always with the same excuse: "I was urged to do it."

My next definite impression is of the political campaign of 1848. The whole country was wildly excited at the approach of the Presidential election. Up to this time the Democrats had had the lion's share of Presidents. The Whigs nominated William Henry Harrison and an unusual effort was made to elect him. It may be truly said that Harrison was sung into office. Ballads in great variety were composed all containing some reference to log cabins, coon skins and hard cider; to pioneer life and his war record. Miniature log cabins were built of poles and mounted on great farm wagons, coon skins were nailed on the outside and a cider barrel was trundled along after it. The little house would hold perhaps twenty people and the wagon was usually drawn by two or three yoke of lusty oxen. In all respects, even to the dress of the young singers, the outfit was made to typify pioneer scenes in a wooded country. Mass meetings were held at many hamlets and not infrequently a half a dozen of these log-cabin cavalcades would be present. With so many lusty singers it was inevitable that a great portion of the exercises should consist in singing these popular and rollicking songs!

The Whigs used ash for their liberty poles in honor of Henry Clay of Ashland, I suppose; while the Democrats used hickory in honor of "Old Hickory," General Jackson. As poles of ash could be procured which were longer and straighter than hickory poles, boys of the Whig persuasion made fun of the hickory poles. This soon created bad blood between the two parties and, not infrequently, the liberty poles were cut down in the night time — now by one party and now by another. This led to the device of inlaying the poles with horse-shoe-nail iron, with old horseshoes and stubs of nails. Even with these precautions the poles sometimes met an untoward fate for they could be bored off near the ground or, with the help of a ladder, they might be sawed off above their armor plate.

The Roberts boys had to have a liberty pole —
for did we not have a beautiful knoll on which to
plant it? We were like the man who purchased a
fine door plate at a bargain and had to build a
house to use it. We had no trouble to find a nice
straight pole in the woods of a size fitted to our
boyish energies; and our pole was never cut nor the
halyards molested, for the flag was nailed to the
mast. I realize now that when that ash liberty
pole was safely planted on that beautiful little hill
above the Lake, and the flag of my country was
cast floating to the breeze that wafted over Old
Cayuga, I had begun to conceive the idea of
patriotism, as well as of party prejudice.

The memories of a somewhat later period which
I am about to set down are not so joyous; they fill
me rather with penitence and with a belated appreciation of my mother's rare patience and kind-
ness. Early in her married life my mother began
to lay by every year a little money for each of her
children; by the time I was about fourteen years
old my portion amounted to about $135, which
was invested in a promissory note drawing seven
per cent simple interest. You can hardly imagine
how bold a face it took to ask my mother for $15
of this money with which to purchase a skiff.
Father's boat had gone to the happy fishing

grounds some time before, and I urged upon her that we really needed a boat, and I showed clearly also — at least it was clear to my boyish mind — that it would be a paying investment because I could hire it out to people who lived back from the Lake and who frequently came down to fish.

When I had persuaded her to give me $15 out of her savings I bought " The Oregon," a trim little craft about fourteen feet long and narrow on the keel. I was not long in discovering that the little sail boats on the Lake could pass me and that rowing, while it might be a manly exercise, was laborious. Thus, although I got my boat and it did prove a paying investment, the money received for its hire never found its way back into the savings fund. For it went to pay for sail cloth, ropes and pulleys and in the loft of the old wagon-house — all secretly, I cut and sewed some sails. I did not fully trust my own seamanship, though I was accustomed to the Lake in its variable moods, so I induced my elder brother to strip and go in swimming with me. Then I bantered him to go with me out into water beyond our depth, upset the skiff and see if both of us could hold to it and ride on that narrow keel. Having done this successfully, we tried to see how far we could push the boat by swimming with our feet while holding on with our hands. After we were thus prepared for squalls by becoming expert upsetters, I put in the sails which were destined to give my mother many an anxious hour. In spite of her expostulation I went out, at first in light wind and near shore, and then in rougher weather, thus putting in practice the advice of the old rhyme:

> "Little boats should keep near shore
> Larger ones may venture more."

But just when I was sure that I had become an experienced sailor the west wind one day laid the little craft on her larboard gunnel and I had all I could do to save myself from drowning. My mother, I think, was never quite easy when I was out in this "tippy" boat and I now realize that I was a most inconsiderate son in that I kept her in a state of constant anxiety. She never forbade me to sail, however, being one of those wise mothers who govern not by edicts but by love.

I have related these particular incidents of my boyhood because they stand out most vividly; but as I look back I think that I was a boy of "incidences," even more than others. I have often studied the problem as to how much liberty and how much restriction children, especially boys, should have; and I have come to the conclusion that the freedom and mother love which I enjoyed saved me from many a temptation and from many sinful acts — they were the sheet anchor of my boyhood days. In after life when I had children of my own it was a great help to think on the wise management of my dear mother and in great measure to put her methods into practice. Inheritance, freedom, environment, restraint, and love — each and all in proper proportion, profoundly affect the lives of children; with me the greatest of these was love. I cannot remember having brazenly disobeyed a direct command of my mother but once; and I cannot express what sorrow I felt for this both then and long afterwards. I have committed offences since which would be considered more blameworthy and which, I trust, have been forgiven — for I often pray to be forgiven for the sins of my youth — but for this sin against my mother I could never forgive myself.

Something should be said of the country in which I spent my boyhood days, for my early environment, I think, had much to do with the trend of my after life. From a little west of

Albany on the east, to and beyond Buffalo on the west, and from the Great Lakes to the northern line of Pennsylvania, was situated a domain of unbounded agricultural capabilities. It was known as the " Lake Country " and it was then considered the garden spot of the New world. It embraced the valley of the Genesee river which at that time was the center of American wheat culture.

It was a region of extraordinary abundance. Noble trees covered the land: oaks, sugar-maples, beeches and a variety of other woods, but the most loved of all in my boyhood was the tall, straight liberty pole, the white ash. A score of lakes diversified the landscape and stored the clear waters of spring and brook and tumbling rivers, not yet contaminated with the sewage of cities. In their clear waters frolicked myriads of edible fish, waiting only for the farmer's boy to come and catch them. The land was overrun with wild animals and with birds while lake and stream swarmed with water-fowl. The soil was full of humus, nitrogen, potash and phosphates of lime; and the larder and storehouse and cellar were filled with abundant and varied food supplies.

I will jot down an incomplete list of the food supplies: on our homestead, for instance, there

were ten varieties of apples, peaches to eat, to dry
and to drink in the form of brandy; plums, pears,
quinces, cherries and grapes; wild strawberries,
blackberries, huckleberries, raspberries — both red
and black — elderberries and cranberries three
miles away in the marsh; and currants and goose-
berries besides, by the bushel.   There were garden
vegetables of all the kinds then known: pumpkins,
squashes, beans and peas from both field and garden; and walnuts, butternuts and hickory nuts to
eat and to sell for spending money.   Plenty of
game, too, especially squirrels, black, red and gray;
pigeons in their season, wild ducks and geese at
the foot of the Lake six miles away and tame ones
in the farmyard.   There was an abundance of fish
to be had by line or seine, to fry or to salt down as
you liked; wood for the cutting — while I now pay
$10 per California cord — of only 100 cubic feet
— or if in stove length, $14 per 100 cubic feet.

But J. G. Holland in his poem, " Bittersweet,"
has described this abundance better than I can do:

" Go with me to the cellar!
　　Look where you step or you'll stumble!
　　Care for your coat or you'll crock it!
　　Down with your crown, man, be humble!
　　Put your head into your pocket,
　　Else something or other will knock it,

Don't hit the jar of cucumbers
Standing on the broad stair!
They have not waked from their slumbers
Since they stood there.

Yet they have lived in a constant jar!
What remarkable sleepers they are!
Turn to the left — shun the wall —
One step more, that is all!
Now we are safe on the ground
I will show you around.
Sixteen barrels of cider
Ripening all in a row!
Those delectable juices
Flowed through the sinuous sluices
Of sweet springs under the orchard,
Climbed into fountains that chained them,
Dripped into cups that retained them,
And swelled till they dropped and we gained them,
When they were gathered and tortured
By passage from hopper to vat,
And fell — every apple crushed flat;
In went the pulp by the scoop-ful,
While the juice flowed by the stoop-ful,
Filling the half of a puncheon
While the men swallowed their luncheon.
Pure grew the stream with the stress
Of the lever and screw
Till the last drops of the press
Were as bright as the dew.
There were the juices spilled;
There were the barrels filled;
Sixteen barrels of cider —
Ripening all in row! "

In that same cellar of ours was cow-butter,
apple-butter and butter-milk; great jars of snow-
white lard, a jar of sausage packed in lard for

summer use; and June butter in stone crocks; a keg of maple syrup made at the close of the run when granulation ceases; and a barrel full of great cakes of tallow. There was always, too, twenty or more six-quart pans of milk, some of which was served at every meal with the cream stirred in.

The clean was separated from the unclean, for there were two cellars, one for the prepared foods and one for the winter supply of fruits and vegetables and salted meats. Besides the vegetables, tubers and fruits, there was vinegar; and by way of meats, pork, hams, beef and fish, all salted away for future needs. As I go into my own cellar now it makes me sad if I chance to think of that cellar of my boyhood: here is only a few paper sacks, a few tinned goods, a quart of milk, six eggs, a peck of potatoes and a pound of bacon which cost thirty-five cents!

Upstairs in my mother's house, there was an ample pantry in which there were jellies and jams, and, best of all, preserves galore —" pound for pound "— mighty filling at 10 p. m., on our return from spelling school on a cold winter night. In a place all by itself in the pantry there was wheat, buckwheat and rye flour, corn-meal and hominy, coarse and fine middlings — the products of ten bushels of grains which had been ground in the water grist-mill where they took every tenth bushel for grinding.

I am near forgetting the loft under the low roof near the chamber where we boys slept. Here were stored bags in numbers, big and little, filled with all kinds of dried fruits and even dried vegetables.

Here too, were strained honey and beeswax, which, all surreptitiously, we nibbled and chewed in weak imitation of our elders who chewed tobacco; and great cakes of maple sugar matrixed in milk pans and piled one upon another in new, clean barrels.

Out in the smoke-house was dried beef — hams and shoulders, bacon and sausage, and unjacketed bull-pouts which had been smoked with corn cobs and hickory chips to give them the desired flavor. Near by stood the great out-door oven in which all sorts of good things were baked, once each week; and they tasted mighty good to me in spite of the fact that I had to split the kindling wood for the oven from the remnants of old basswood rails. As if this were not enough great pits of apples, cabbages and beets, turnips and carrots, were buried in the garden for spring use, for many of the things in the cellar would in time become wilted and specked. No pen can do justice to this land of abundance though half a score of hungry children could.

With such an abundant food supply and with so rich a soil, every living creature, man included, had a strong bony and muscular structure. So among the many things for which I am thankful is the circumstance that my boyhood was spent in that land of well-balanced plenty before the cream of the soil had been filched from it. Dr. Thomas D. Wood, formerly the Professor of Hygiene at Stanford University, now at Columbia University, Teachers College, once informed me that the students of Stanford University who were born and reared in the State of California were markedly taller and heavier on the average than those from the East. What complexions, what bloom on the cheeks, these western women have, where hats are dispensed with most of the time during the nine summer months! What a firm, elastic stride, that carries them over the foothills and up the mountain side, through tangled glen and stony canyon with the minimum of fatigue and the maximum of joy that only comes from reserve physical power. Unquestionably the quality of foods gives size and strength, health and vigor, both to mankind and to domesticated animals.

In a valley in Italy it has been noted by travellers that the people were prematurely decrepit, due to the lack of the normal bony structure. The analysis of hay, given below shows conclusively a serious lack of bone-making material, and if it was lacking in the hay, then we must conclude that nearly all of the foods of the people were also deficient.

	COMPOSITION OF HAY, POUNDS IN 1,000			
	Ash	Nitrogen	Phosphate	Potash
Best American meadow hay, 141 samples.....	71.4	19.2	4.8	15.2
European meadow hay, where men and animals are weak-boned and under-sized......	45.5	14.4	2.3	12.0

It is evident that American farmers cannot continue to deplete the land of its most valuable constituents without endangering the size and the physical power of coming generations. I trust that the Agricultural Colleges and Experiment Stations will teach them how to restore the land to its pristine richness, so that our posterity may not be

of so slight and delicate a type and the alimentary
canal so undeveloped that they cannot bear the
burdens of this strenuous modern world. "Tell
me what you eat and I will tell you what manner
of man you are," is an old saying. But tell me
what the soil is, and I will tell you the quality of
the men and animals which will be produced from
the foods raised upon it.

I see those healthy country girls of the early
nineteenth century, yet; dressed in "store goods"
— calico or gingham — protected by white or
colored aprons, with a little home-made lace to
set off their rounded necks and with quite undis-
torted forms; although work had made their hands
large and strong their faces revealed a well
nourished body, a cheerful temper and the habits
of right living. If the world was not better in
those days, it was certainly more natural. We
of the first half of the last century had more manual exercise than our grandchildren but the pity
bestowed on us for our hard pioneer conditions
might better be given to the shop and factory
workers of today.

I have been a pioneer in three fertile new states
in my time, but I have yet to see a country so
liberally supplied with the bounties of life, or a

people so sturdy, productive and self-reliant, as the inhabitants of the Lake Country in New York, in the second quarter of the nineteenth century. My uncle, Thomas Burroughs, my father Aaron P. Roberts, and our nearest neighbor, Michael Ritter, owned adjoining farms together comprising between four and five hundred acres. There were born to these three heads of families thirty-two children, only one of whom died before reaching the age of thirty, and that one lost his life in the battle of Bull Run. These children were all strong and capable; some of them rose to places of modest distinction, all of them were law-abiding and temperate in habits of living and thought, and most of them received all or nearly all of their school education in the schools of the district and in the nearby-academies. Besides those mentioned, twelve other families resided in our school district but I would not have it inferred that each of these furnished an equal quota to the school, for if so, there would have been at least eighty pupils while there were, in fact, only sixty on the rolls even in winter.

During the last fifteen years the occupiers of these three homesteads just mentioned have furnished only two pupils for this school a part of

the time, while the whole number of pupils ranges
in summer from eight to twelve.   I cannot explain
altogether the causes of this change in District
No. 8. The farms are not deserted, only somewhat less productive and somewhat more expensive
to till; but I believe that the low price of farm
products, especially of wheat, our staple crop, has
had much to do with this decadence, since for
more than a quarter of a century wheat has sold
on an average in New York for less than $1 per
bushel, while the *cost* of production under the local
conditions has become one dollar and a quarter or
more.   It should be remembered that wheat sold
in 1818 for $3.00 per bushel in this very locality.

I have recently been making an extended investigation of the cost of producing a bushel of wheat
in various parts of the country and it is my opinion
that the lack of profit in wheat growing has been
an important factor in the decline of the birth rate
and at the same time it has been the cause of the
westward migration of the more adventurous
members of the population.   Nevertheless the land
from which products have for so long been sold
for less than the true cost of production — figured
at a fair wage and with deduction for loss of producing power — is still worthy of the plowman's

steel. Now that consumption is out-running production it may be hoped that the land and its owners will come into their own again — when people
have a waiting appetite the men who hold the loaf
are masters of the situation.

We have not yet realized how profoundly food
supply and demand have affected our national life
nor how it is destined to affect us in the future.
The central thought in those long years at Cornell University and the faith which held me true
to my work, was that food is the first requirement
of life. Some morning these United States will
wake up with a sharp appetite for breakfast and
then the farmer may have something to say as to
the price that shall be given for his products —
if he can partially eliminate the middleman. I
have long expected that the era of high-priced
foods would come upon us, and now that it is here
I rejoice over it. For when a product is sold in
the market for less than a fair profit over the cost
of production, both producer and consumer suffer.

It was only about fifteen years ago that a farmer
brought a wagon-box full of potatoes to Ithaca
which he could neither sell nor trade for groceries.
Disgusted beyond measure, he slipped out the end-
board of the wagon, cracked his whip and drove

rapidly through the streets and up west hill; long before he had reached the top his potatoes had disappeared and, gazing back, he remarked: "I couldn't look those overfed city chaps in the face while those beautiful potatoes were staring at me with their innocent eyes." This is an extreme illustration of one of the causes which has driven the country boy from the farm and which has also led the farmer to neglect to keep up the productive ability of the soil.

There is one great and ever present natural law which modifies reproduction, at least in mammals. If food is scarce and environment unkind the age of puberty is postponed and reproduction is limited, as among Indians and other primitive races in severe climates and where food is insufficient. The Esquimo has not been destroyed by war and not until recently decimated by diseases, yet throughout the ages they have multiplied but slowly. If environment is made comfortable — not luxurious — and an abundance of wholesome, not too concentrated food is provided, reproduction tends to rise in proportion; while at the other extreme, if environment is too easy, too luxurious, reproduction again declines. This is a law as true of the genus homo as it is of the genus *sus scrofa*.

As to materials for clothing in my boyhood there was scarcely less abundance than there was of food supplies. The woods were full of small fur-bearing animals; the beef hides were waiting to be exchanged for leather; the wool, both white and black, to be shorn from the heavy sheep; feathers and down to be plucked when ripe from the noisy geese and ducks; and better than all, the flax in its bloom.

The children were well and warmly clad in stoutly made if not always perfectly fitting clothes. One of my earliest memories is of a pair of new shoes which I proudly put on in the kitchen where they had been made by a travelling cobbler. The uppers were made from my father's, or perhaps my eldest brother's, boot-tops — for men always wore *boots* while boys, girls and women wore shoes which were sometimes made from cast-off boot-tops. The art of splitting leather was then unknown. The travelling shoemaker might be with us two or three weeks in the fall or early winter, and he was very welcome, especially to the boys. While he told us lots of new stories and brought to us the flavor of the outside world, he also gave us a chance to lay in a store of waxed ends with which to sew leather covers on our home-made baseballs which were of woolen yarn ravelled from the tops of discarded stockings. Although the tops of those long, hand-knit stockings were re-footed, often more than once, the time came when they were not worth repairing and then they were handed over to the boys. Sometimes, I must confess we did not even wait for the re-footing.

I remember I went out to try my new shoes in the new-fallen snow. The older boys knew, as I did not, that new shoe soles are a slippery, treacherous underpinning, so they and the dog went along to see the fun. After I had gone down several times they set the dog on me and then the real fun began, for as I got up the dog would push me over with his playful antics. Queer, isn't it, that I can remember every detail of those shoes, the mischievous joy of my brothers and even the color of the dog, yet I forget many of the transactions of yesterday!

My father always wore a grayish-colored, tall stiff hat in shape much like the silk hats of the present day. In the top of the crown he carried letters and other valuable papers — I say other, because letters were then precious — which were held down or up by a highly colored silk or cotton handkerchief. His coat, with collar built high and reinforced with buckram, was a long cut-a-way

—" Shadbelly." The vest was long and ample; the breeches were loose (held up by knit suspenders, even the buttonholes being knit in) and cut in a fashion far more modest than modern trousers. His high shirt collar was lightly starched and fell naturally over a stiff, high stock, held in place by a buckle.

When riding out of doors in winter every man was provided with a soft knit muffler a foot wide and nearly two yards long. Muffs were common while the foot-stove was a necessary comfort for any long drive. Most men, however, did not wear the stiff silk hat but caps made of cloth, or coon or squirrel skin. While these were worn by boys also I cannot remember ever to have had one; for in my time we could purchase " cap-peaks " which were stitched in between the lining and the body of the home-made cap of cloth, perhaps the well-preserved part of an old coat. In winter we boys all wore knit caps with a flowing tassel at the top. For dress-up on Sunday in summer men wore white linen pants as late as 1850. Our underwear was tow, linen or wool according to season, but by 1850 cotton had come to be generally used.

It is certainly marvellous how in one generation, the New York pioneers changed from homespun

clothes, coonskin caps and shoes made from boot-
tops, to Congress gaiters, patent leather shoes,
" Prince Albert " or black long frock coats and
silk hats — for these were my Sunday and party
garments when I reached the age of twenty-one.
In the same generation the farmers gave up the
ox-cart and farm wagon and began to ride in top
carriages which cost from $125 to $175. We
were not unlike other fortunate peoples, settled in
a district of unbounded natural resources which
required relatively little skill to transform into
articles of use and luxury.

But some of this transformation demanded both
skill and hard work. Did you ever pull flax?
Linum usitatissimum? That word may be a jaw-
breaker but be assured it is not half so hard for
jaws as pulling flax was for my back! Just about
the time we ceased to raise flax a machine was
invented for pulling it. Of course we could have
cut it with the grain cradle but the fibre would have
then been too short for use. The little sheaves
of flax were threshed in the early fall by beating
them on a large flat stone tilted at about an angle
of 35 degrees; afterward the threshed material
was spread one to two inches thick in well-ordered
swaths on the grass of some meadow. In from

three to four weeks, during which it had been turned several times, it had become sufficiently rotted and was then bound in large bundles and stored in the barn. Early in the following spring, on some crisp, windy day, a portion of the straw was spread out in the sun and wind preparatory to being run through the brake. The lower part of the brake consisted of four hardwood boards set in a heavy frame about four feet long, each sharpened on the upper edge and fastened, closer in front than at the back, in two blocks of wood which were furnished with suitable legs. The upper part was made in a similar manner except that there were only three sharpened boards set in smaller blocks and so placed that the upper bars would mis-match with the lower ones. The rear block or head served also as a hinge which permitted the front end to be raised or lowered.

The operator, with as much straw as he could hold in his left hand, raised the brake, thrust the flax first under the rear end where the spaces were largest between the sharpened boards, then let the top or swinging part of the brake fall upon it. This process repeated caused the woody parts to drop away from the fine fibre. The flax had still to be " scutched," that is, dressed over a sharpened board with a wooden sword, which further removed the woody fibre. Then it was hatcheled or "heckled" which carried the operation of eliminating the woody fibre to a finish. The material which remained was called linen, and a hank of it looked not unlike a fluffy, light-blond switch of hair. That part which the hatchel combed out of the linen at first was "tow," suitable for making ropes; and that combed out later was spun into yarn and used as filling in making tow and linen cloth.

The process by which wool was prepared for weaving was less laborious. The wool was first washed on the backs of the sheep and the day on which that was done was looked forward to by the children with joyous anticipation. Then it was tub-washed and picked apart by hand. A part of the white wool was mixed with about one-fourth of its bulk of black wool to make sheep's gray cloth or yarn; while the balance was left in its natural color. If pure black or variegated colors were desired the yarn was dyed. The wool was then treated with melted lard and picked a second time making it ready for the cards, which by skillful manipulation formed it into rolls ready for spinning.

In addition to the instruments for preparing the flax there was much other machinery: a rope-yarn wheel, for my father made all the rope used on the farm which was not a little; a tow and flax wheel; the large wheel for spinning wool; the swifts for forming the yarn into skeins; and the quill wheel. In my time most of the weaving was done by professional weavers at their homes at a stipulated price per yard. In later years the wool prepared for the cards was sent to the factory where it was transformed either into yarn for stockings and mittens or into cloth. At a still later period the unprepared wool was traded for cloth and yarn.

In the fall, my mother would go to Seneca Falls and purchase cloth for the grown-ups and buttons and linings. Then with a great roll of sheep's gray and a sleigh or wagon-load of children she proceeded to the nearest approved tailor where we were all measured for our outside winter clothing. Then there came to the house two or three seamstresses who would make up the cut-out garments in from two to four weeks. Sometimes they were directed to cut off some of the old trousers legs above the knee, rip the seams and re-sew them with the fronts of the legs behind and the backs in front. That deferred the time when someone had

" to piece a patch, to patch a patch, to patch a pair of trousers-knee."

With ribbed mittens, long thick stockings, new shoes and over-socks for warmth, a large fluffy muffler, a new suit warmly lined and often padded, we met the on-coming winter blasts without a shiver, although we seldom wore overcoats.

Being only a farm kid I cannot remember distinctly what the girls and women wore. Their underwear was of necessity of tow and linen in summer and some kind of thick wool in winter. They wore linsey-woolsey skirts, while their outer garments were of wool, home-produced, or calico or gingham or, for the best dress of the well-to-do women, silk. It was the invariable custom for the purchaser of a farm to make a present of a dress to the wife or eldest daughter of the seller. If the amount of the realty was large, a silk dress; if small then a gingham dress, discharged the obligation demanded by the custom of the country.

EDUCATION

My mother taught me to read and to figure up to and including the multiplication table. Often my lesson was learned before the winter daylight broke by the great fireplace, while she was knitting stockings — or socks and mittens — for a score of feet and legs, and as many hands. For many years there was only one pair of hands to do all these things, but the stockings were always symmetrically narrowed down at the toe and heel and the thumbs of the mittens fitted almost as perfectly as a modern glove.

Like all the other children of the neighborhood I was kept steadily in school both winter and summer until I was about twelve years of age; after that I helped on the farm in summer and went to school in winter. In *our* home there was always a school atmosphere and in winter the great kitchen was turned into an evening school-room, the older children helping the younger ones in their studies. Sometimes in the spring when the land was not yet fit for tilling and my brothers' schools were closed, the carpet was removed from the parlor and a cousin of ours — a graduate of Yale — was employed to teach us all. This extra home school continued for a month or more but it was always closed as soon as the land was fit for the plow.

In the district school house which was located on a stony hog-back and which has long since been destroyed, I learned at least one valuable lesson.

Long writing tables were arranged around three sides of the room against the wall. In front of these were seats for the larger pupils and in front of these seats were the backless benches for the kids — in those heathen days we called them "trucklebed trash." These benches were made of heavy oak slabs with four, straddling, pin-like legs, and were placed just in front of the great ten-plate heating stove. When it got too hot the little fellows crowded to the end of the bench and not infrequently someone got shoved off onto the floor. Then came the laugh and the reckoning — "for going to sleep and falling off the bench." The boys caught me napping once and the teacher awakened me by blistering the seat of my breeches. After that I swung my feet against the big side bench and braced; and discovered for the first time what happens when an irresistible force meets an immovable body — the irresistible received just punishment and the immovable escaped. Ever since then I have known enough to brace when things or men scrouge.

I used to envy a big boy who had purloined a broken-bottom Windsor chair from the kitchen at home, and recovering it with a soft woolly sheepskin, had placed it in a cozy corner of the school room, while I had to sit on the soft side of an oak slab, in front of that stove as hot as the lower regions, with my feet at least four inches from the floor. In summer time my legs served as roosts for flies while I was planning how to catch that chipmunk which had his hole just six panels from the bars which opened into the cow pasture. No wonder I was regarded as the intellectual black-sheep of our family!

The details of my early school life will scarcely interest you since my studies did not interest me, but all nine of the children in our family were successful teachers at one time or another, and notwithstanding I was the slow one, I also made the " riffle " at last. This exceptional interest in education may be attributed to my mother's ambi-tion. I once heard her say: " I received a better education than my parents did, and come what may, I am determined to give my children a better education than I have." And because she worked and saved and sacrificed to make her words come true, I have striven to do the same for the next generation.

When I was about fourteen years old I had to go back into the summer school because I had fallen behind — having become, as they said, too fond of the lake and the woods and the chipmunks.

Two consecutive terms under a rarely good teacher, took me far beyond vulgar fractions, the point at which I had usually arrived when school closed every spring; and by the end of the next winter term I could exclaim with one of Edward Eggleston's characters: "Lay there, Old Pike-Davis and Thompson's Higher and show me an example that I cannot do!"

The educational facilities and the teaching were uniformly good in our locality, according to the standards of the time, although both education and religion were informed more with the letter than the spirit. There was an atmosphere of cultural and intellectual activities, stimulated not only by frequent spelling schools, debating clubs, and singing schools, but also by evening gatherings where difficult mental examples were propounded — riddles, charades and rebusses, catch-word sayings, and highly moral as well as foolish and laughable things, both in prose and rhyme.

Here are a few of these old puzzles on which we whetted our minds:

A HARD ONE

I am disposed to plant a grove
To satisfy the maid I love:
This ample grove must be composed
Of nineteen trees in nine straight rows;

Five in a row I there must place
Or ne'er expect to see her face.
Ye men of art, lend me your aid
To satisfy this curious maid!

AN EASIER ONE

" Somebody take the basket and bring me just one
apple from the orchard. How many apples must you
start with so that you can leave half the apples you
have and half an apple more at the first gate, and at
the second gate do the same, and at the third and last
gate repeat the division of apples as before and bring
me the one apple that is left."

FOR THE LITTLE BOYS WHO LOVE FISHING

" If a herring and a half cost a cent and a half, what
will five herring and a half cost? "
" If the third of six be three, what will the fourth of
twenty be? "

HARVESTING APPLES AND PEARS

" There was a man who had no eyes
And he went out to view the skies;
He saw an apple tree had apples on,
He took no apples off nor left no apples on."

" Twelve men riding by, twelve pears hanging high;
Each man took a pear and left eleven hanging there."

" Spell ' sink ' (cinque), meaning five."

Then there were Aesop's Fables in rhyme — I
could fill pages with them; and with a multitude
of little " tangles " which had been handed down
from the time of the Pilgrims. One of the most

laughable entertainments was a debate — in imitation of our elders — conducted by a dozen boys on the subject: "Which is the worst — a scolding wife or a smoky chimney?"

This may appear silly to the reader, but it was a part of our life, of my life. Crude as it was, it taught me to love and to commit to memory many things, sad and gay, solid and trivial, which were expressed in rhyme; and it taught me also to speak somewhat easily on my feet. I understand that in some of the schools to-day pupils are not allowed to learn the alphabet or to memorize the multiplication table. I presume this accounts for the fact that many college students, in multiplying a number by twelve, do so by first multiplying by the two and then by the one, instead of by a single operation. The men of my day got there quicker — as, for instance, Mr. Henry B. Lord, the Cashier of the Bank of Ithaca, who had learned the multiplication table up to the twentieth line and could add two columns at a time, accurately and swiftly. The new method may account too for the fact that so many pupils in the modern schools have difficulty in finding a word in the dictionary — they have not learned the letters of the alphabet consecutively.

3

Within one or two days' drive of our town there were ten academies, perhaps, of a grade equal to the small colleges of to-day: and, while they did not teach as many things as the colleges do now, I am certain that they gave better training and were more insistent upon good work.

Very few boys went to college, so that all the higher education most of us had was secured in these academies. I base my judgment of them on the class of men they sent forth. By the time I was fitted to enter an academy the State had organized normal departments in them; and by pledging myself to devote a reasonable portion of my time after graduation to teaching, I obtained free tuition. I certainly kept my agreement, for I taught seven winters in public and common schools and over thirty-three years in college and University in the course of my after life.

It was the custom in large and ambitious families to keep one or more children at some academy, at least during the winter, provisioning them weekly from the farm. As rooms and fuel were cheap and the students did their own cooking, this was a satisfactory and inexpensive way of educating children far beyond the common school. But even the common schools were more advanced and more generally attended than now. Indeed, these pioneer people laid almost as much stress upon "schooling" as upon manual dexterity and willingness to work.

I recall an instance which proves this point: three substantial farmers were elected school trustees and two of them drove twelve miles to interview a teacher of wide reputation. The teacher said that he presumed the salary he asked would be too high, considering the wages they were accustomed to paying. One trustee — an unlettered Pennsylvania Dutchman — said to the other: "Burroughs, the folks won't stand that salary, but can't you and I pay the excess out of our own pockets?" And they did! The grandson of that Dutchman was superintendent of the schools of Stockton, California, for many years, and two of his great-grandsons are distinguished graduates of leading Universities.

OUR PLEASURES

Was farm life lonely and monotonous in such a country and in those pioneer days? By no means! In fact it was most enjoyable — busy and rollicking, just what a country lad enjoys. It is true there was much work, but there was also much fun to balance it, for both old folks and children knew how to turn work into play. Certainly husking corn was not work when it was done by the light of lanterns hung from the rough beams of the great barns where the horses wondered and blinked at the unwonted scene, and where the soft shadows mellowed the rosy but modest blushes of a bevy of girls who were all on the *qui vive* for the expected tussle for a kiss when one of the boys should find the coveted red ear. Nor was the aftermath of the husking bee — a glorious supper and a moonlight walk — laborious. It could scarcely be called work when a score of young men on a moonlight night cut a small field of overripe grain for a sick neighbor and afterward went to some farmhouse, or to where the brook met the lake, to partake of a picnic meal served by hands not oversoft but willing and competent.

I remember mornings when the snow came with the sting of a whip over the clear, cold, blue lake. Jump on the ox-sled with me and go to the woods, sitting on the rave, and hanging your feet over on the outside! Don't touch the chain with your hands, for this is a morning when " cold steel tastes sweet ". The whole wood is covered with virgin snow, which comes showering down on you

if you so much as touch a limb with the whip.
Look at the delicate tracery in the snow left by the
tiny wood-folk when getting their breakfast! Ah,
here is the pile of wood — brush off the snow with
your thick woolen mittens! There, we have it all
loaded but those two sticks — look out now! for
there is a nest of wood-mice under them, and if
one runs up your leg under your trousers, won't
you run and scream and slap! Looking back from
the standpoint of modern comforts and the milder
California climate, one is inclined to pity those
New York pioneers for the hardships which they
endured; but the snowy winters had their compen-
sations when we battled with a full stomach and
warm clothing.

On cold, still moonlight nights, when the crys-
talled ice covered everything, our sleds creaked as
they sped over the glistening surface down the hill
and far out on the ice-bound lake; and our skates
rang sharply on the newly-formed ice. When
nature was in her milder mood of summer, we
stripped to two garments and lolled in the shadow
of the huge sycamore tree which grew just at the
water's edge, beyond the shelter-house of our sail-
boat, *The Oregon*. There we would lie watching
the sails taut with the soft south wind, or flapping

idly against the stays in a calm; or we followed
the steamer with its long line of canal boats laden
with the wealth of field and wood for the distant
market. Sometimes a passenger boat came in close
to shore to avoid a strong, westerly wind. With
what anxiety we watched for the cloud of black
smoke and the sound of her laborious breathing,
and the first wave that struck the shore made by
her lightning speed — as we thought it — while
the foam rose from her bows. As I lay there on
the bank I used to wonder what was beyond my
little horizon. I longed for a wider life and for a
more intimate knowledge of the great world, which
seemed to me to have no limits; and it was this
unsatisfied desire of my youth that led me to
travel far and wide when I became older.

Since all the children on a farm helped with the
work more or less from their childhood, it may be
guessed that we did not have so much time for
games as children do nowadays. The most general, then as now, was baseball, which differed
from the modern game in several features. The
ball was then reasonably soft. It might be thrown
at a runner if he was off his base, by anyone of the
opposing side, and if he were hit, he was out.
Strikes and hits and fouls were the same as now;

but it was a more dignified game in that it consisted of dodging rather than sliding to bases. We waxed as enthusiastic as boys do now, but such a thing as betting on an amateur game was quite unknown.

RELIGIOUS LIFE OF THE NEIGHBORHOOD

The nearest church in my boyhood was at Mc-Duffietown, a hamlet made up of half a dozen houses and three small shops about two miles from East Varick. At that time the Methodist spirit — for this was a Methodist church — was so intense that I do not think that a Unitarian, or Universalist or Roman Catholic could have lived there without being ostracized. The people tributary to this church were, however, not all church members; perhaps not more than one-half of the heads of families and two-thirds of the younger people over twelve years of age were communicants. But, as there was no other church within five or six miles, the congregation was generally quite large.

Scarcely a winter passed without a " protracted " meeting, and these services were extremely noisy, what with the stentorian preaching, loud praying, wild singing and shouting. The excitement not infrequently culminated when some overemotional

convert fainted while " getting the spirit." Such
a revival was a highly entertaining place for the
youths of a wide countryside in search of fun.
Then, as now, there were many who came to church
to be entertained rather than instructed; but a few
came to entertain as well as to be entertained, for
all attended — whether church members or not —
the revival meetings. While the noise and excitement were going on in the front seats, many mischievous acts were perpetrated in the back seats.
The legs of the great box heating stove, which had
a very long pipe for additional warmth, were set
up on loose bricks, and these could easily be worked
from under by the foot. After working a brick
out of place the culprit, with others in the secret,
would start for a cooler place and immediately the
red-hot stove would topple over and a portion of
the pipe would come down. This stopped the services and created a wild panic, but the cause of the
disaster was seldom discovered.

Although this was the most serious prank I ever
witnessed, it was by no means the only one. If for
any reason the shouting and praying in the front
seats ceased for a moment, the scuffling and loud
talking of the unregenerate in the back seats would
be heard and somebody was likely to be led out

by the collar. Other mischief makers would follow him out and then there might be a scrub horse-race or a foot-race outside; or a string of light sleighs might be driven rapidly around the church as though around a race track. All this was generally the work of a half dozen wild young fellows while I with a score of others looked on, and I confess, enjoyed it all. The church leaders must have been sorely tried, for they were good men, or at any rate they led irreproachable lives in the sight of the world. Most heads of families who were church members, held daily family prayers and the preacher, when he made his parochial visits, always prayed with the household.

At the period of which I am writing, 1840 to 1850, converts were given their choice of the mode of baptism, that is, by sprinkling or immersion, and the latter was usually chosen. On some Sunday in early spring a great throng would assemble on the shore of Cayuga Lake to witness the immersions. The Methodist Church did not at this time lay great stress on the manner of baptism but it did anathematize jewelry, bright ribbons and even furs when worn by women, and many a new convert discarded all of them. No one was allowed to speak from the pulpit except a minister, and singing schools were only permitted under the strictest supervision.

About 1870, this old barn-like church having become dilapidated, a broader-minded pastor made an attempt to interest outsiders in building a new one. My uncle, Thomas Burroughs, whom I had never seen at church, coöperated most cordially and energetically in building the new church. I was, by that time, a Professor at Cornell University and was appealed to for contributions and responded three times as did some other non-residents. At the time the church was finally dedicated there was still a debt on it and I, thinking that curiosity, if not my reputation, would draw an audience, offered to deliver an address, the proceeds of which should go toward reducing the debt. The older people of that community had known me as a crude, tow-headed lad and might have been willing to pay twenty-five cents to hear me, but the trustees still held to the old-time narrow views and refused my offer because I was not an ordained minister!

The religion of that early day was emotional rather than spiritual, and hell-fire was more preached than Christian living; but in spite of dogmatic narrowness, the Christian atmosphere of that old church helped much to hold that vigorous, fun-loving, intemperate, pioneer people within reasonable bounds, and sometimes it made heroes of them.

AGRICULTURAL AND ECONOMIC CONDITIONS

I remember not only the outdoor pleasures, the singing schools, and the revival meetings, but also the working life when no fun relieved the monotonous tasks. Our farm consisted of 100 acres of good land and was a mile long and fifty rods wide, on the lake side. Its inconvenient shape was the result of a well-conceived plan to have as many farm-house sites as possible near the lake shore. Originally, it was covered with a prodigious growth of hardwoods — mostly beech and sugar maple. The slope from the back end of the farm to the lake was gentle and regular, there was not much rock and the newly-cleared land produced a wide range of edible fruits and plants. The soil, however, contained too much clay for easy tillage, especially when moisture was lacking; but it was not a stubborn soil if tilled at the right time and not tramped when too moist.

The timber and wood was disappearing so rapidly by the time I was half-grown that body cord-wood could be sold on the lake bank for $2.50 and $3 per cord and the last of the clearings therefore increased the receipts from the farm. In the spring, after school was closed we boys prepared the household wood, but we dodged the more laborious task of cutting cord-wood in the forest. To have it cut at first cost sixty cents and later seventy-five cents per cord. On Saturdays not infrequently, I had to draw the cord-wood down to the bank of the lake. A cord of green body sugar-maple weighs about two tons, and since the sled was arranged for a cord and that was considered a load I, boy-like, proposed to haul as large loads as the neighbors and I sometimes got stuck. I was too small for such heavy labor and the team was weak from standing unused during the winter, so we sometimes stopped before we got fairly started unless I had taken the precaution to place some small round sticks under the sled before loading. If the start was successful still there was danger, for the lane often had one-sided snowbanks and the fun of upsetting never fully balanced the work of reloading, as a singing school upset did.

Did you ever plow a new clearing? Well, if you ever did without using any strong language I would like to take you by the hand and make you a farmer *emeritus*. The meanest work of all, perhaps, was piling and burning the brush. When things went badly we had a saying which ran in this wise: "It will all come right when the clearing is burned." The effect of these laborious struggles upon a lot of boys too long in the back for such hardships, showed later — as I will presently relate.

Those sturdy pioneers with ax and fire-brand let the sun in on many fair acres and land prices began to go up by leaps and bounds — from twenty to thirty and even to forty dollars per acre. The earliest settlers gratified that irresistible desire for land which they had inherited from a long line of Anglo-Saxon ancestors; but my father, seeing no chance of acquiring more land at a low price in New York to give each of his sons a farm, went to Michigan and purchased nearly 500 acres at $2.50 per acre. After a time we traded forty acres of it for a chaff-piler threshing machine with which we occasionally threshed for the neighbors; but we soon came to the conclusion that it was dirty business. Taxes were paid on this Michigan land for more than thirty years; and we did our share toward the erection of three school houses — for no sooner was one school house built than the district lines were changed and our land found itself again among the heathen. Then we were taxed for draining swamp-land; then for a great ditch to drain the roadway. It was the old story of taxing non-residents in season and out. Before the land was finally disposed of I found out that cord-wood could be sold in Chicago at such a price as to make it profitable to clear the land. As our tract was situated not far from Lake Michigan, I supposed that transportation would be cheap. But I discovered that the railroads would not transport a cord of wood to the boat landing because every cord moved out of the district tended to increase the price of their own supply. This land was sold at last for about $25 per acre and not one tree ever felt the keen edge of a Roberts' ax. Thus fathers propose and children dispose!

If someone in those pioneer days had shown the farmers of Varick that by clearing the best half of each farm and by producing only two-thirds as much as on the whole, they could realize more net income and avoid much hard labor, there would still be a goodly portion of virgin forest left and those farms would now be worth twice as much as they are. Through short-sighted, unintelligent farm practice, for the most part, the markets during the first seventy-five years of the nineteenth century were glutted with the most easily produced farm products and with the woods of the forest so that prices were often reduced to a point below reasonable profit and the soil was depleted besides.

In addition to this loss, as soon as the roots had decayed the drainage channels left thereby filled with silt, the soil lost something of its humus and the fields became too wet for early and easy tillage. An effort was then made to improve the condition of the soil by cutting rather narrow, shallow ditches which were partly filled with broken stone and then covered with straw, and the straw with dirt. But these soon became obstructed and were then replaced by deeper stone ditches, constructed by laying, on both sides of the ditch, small roundish stone from the lake shore, of four to six inches diameter; and upon these, broad, flattish stone to make an open throat. Finish stones were then chinked in, after which the straw and dirt cover followed. These larger drains were fairly efficient but in time required frequent repairs. Finally about 1855, drain-pipe and horse-shoe tile became available and the wettest parts of the land were under-drained for the third time. Only a faint idea can be given of the labor in clearing and draining necessary in those days to bring a farm up to a high power of production.

Meanwhile vast quantities of easily available plant food were being removed through the crops without any adequate consideration of the labor, skill, investment and plant-food involved; for such profit as was apparently secured was only obtained by selling the cream of the soil and our labor and skill at too low a price. I hold that no profit should be counted until a sufficient sinking fund has been set apart to tide over misfortunes and old age; for if parents have to be supported in their age by their children, it is evident that they have not earned, at least have not received, a life-supply of food and clothing — a pitiful result, indeed, for a life-time of industry, economy and honest living.

If a man is fortunate enough to fill out his three score and five years, he should earn enough in forty adult years to pay for the cost of his living during the first twenty and for the last five, as well as for the period of his active, productive life. Most

of us do not do this; we live on comfortably only
because of our inheritance of books containing
knowledge, of devices of a thousand kinds which
save labor and which vastly increase our productive power; because of houses and roads and farms
and money; because in short, of the accumulations
of the successful few who have preceded us.

The home farm came to be worth, ultimately,
$85 per acre; during the war it rose to more than
$100 per acre — in depreciated greenbacks — and
now has fallen to $50 per acre. It is evident
enough why the Roberts boys did not take kindly
to the noble profession of agriculture; and why
so many farm boys are no longer willing to farm
unless, perchance, they can secure virgin, treeless,
stoneless land at $1.25 per acre — which is only a
little more than the present price of a bushel of
wheat — or can have it given to them outright.
Happily the days when the farmers were spend-
thrift of natural resources are coming to an end;
and happily, too, a well educated boy may now
find a liberal reward on the farm for the efforts
made in harmony with Nature's modes of action
and in conformity with modern science and approved practices. But it is not surprising that
modern young men do not take kindly to repairing

waste places and to correcting the mistakes of their forefathers.

Having generalized somewhat on soil robbery and soil renaisscence, it is time to return to farm details in Central New York. For many years there were two weeds which caused great annoyance and incessant labor to keep in check. As soon as the fields were cleared the Canada thistle — *carvinces* — found a foothold and, the land being rich and mellow, it required great persistency to keep it in check. The usual rotation was corn or fallow, oats, barley or flax, then wheat; clover for one year and for pasture one. This was followed by a three-to-five-plowing summer fallow, if the thistles were scattered over most of the field; if they were in restricted patches, these were plowed frequently during the year the field was in pasture, thus to a great extent avoiding an idle year.

Even with all these precautions some thistles would appear in the grain and the sheaves of wheat had to be touched most gingerly; and, fight as steadily as we might, they were never wholly eradicated. In those days I used to feel, while cuffing the soil back and forth with an imperfect plow so many times during those long summer days, that I was the particular victim of the pestiferous

Canada thistle. I revisited the old farm in 1904
and I recognized some of those same thistles that
used to torment my bare feet and aching legs, but
they were not so rank and vicious as they had been
when the land was new and rich.

Pigeon-weed, redroot — corn gromwell — was
very common and was known by the first name in
our region. Two explanations were given for the
name: the one arose from the fact that the seeds
looked wonderfully like a pigeon's head, while the
other and more obvious one was that the pigeons
had brought in the seed. During fall and spring
enormous flocks of these birds passed over the
country in migration to and from their breeding
ground. It is known that pigeons, if they have
partaken of undesirable food and afterward find
better, disgorge the first and feed upon that which
is more satisfactory. Stumps and trees left for
shade, furnished alighting places from which these
birds could view the grain which had not been
covered by the primitive wooden-toothed harrow.
They " coughed up " their previous meal — as the
college boys would say — and gobbled down the
precious seed grain. The weed was seen at first
about stumps and under the trees where the pigeons
alighted, but it soon became distributed over the

whole field. We had no way of eradicating it but
to hand-pull it; in extreme cases I have known it
to cost $5 per acre to pull it from a single wheat
crop. I myself once hired out to pull this weed
at fifty cents a day; but I soon abandoned the job
for my wages scarcely sufficed to purchase liniment
enough to cure my backache.

We got rid of the pigeon weed finally by changing the crop rotation. The birds that brought it,
however, served us both for food and sport. To
catch them a net, twelve feet broad and thirty
feet long, was laid in a rope-like mass near the
woods — on the north side in the spring and on
the south in the fall — and so arranged that it
could be quickly raised, spread and brought to the
ground by means of small ropes. Two pigeons
having been caught, the lids of their eyes were
stitched together; to the leg of one — the flier —
a long string was attached and the other was
fastened to a stool which could be raised or lowered two or three feet by means of a cord from
the bush-house. In front of the net the ground
was baited with wheat. When the pigeons were
heard coming over the woods up went the flier, into
the bush-house dodged the boy. When the flier
got to the end of its string it would hover as
pigeons do when they are about to alight to eat.

When the attention of the flock had been caught and its flight arrested the stool pigeon was made to hover by being suddenly raised and lowered. If the flock became mistrustful — pigeons have a way of snapping their wings when frightened — it took quick work to net them and some always got away, but that did not matter as other flocks were certain to follow. Seneca County is now entirely deserted by the wild pigeon and the pigeonweed is no longer a serious menace; but the Canada thistle, like taxes, still puts in an appearance every year.

Wild geese and ducks seldom came to the fields but dwelt in the marshes at the foot of the Lake. The chipmunks, the crows and the brown cut-worm sometimes did much injury to seed and growing plants of maize. The two former have long departed but the latter still remains in fields which are not under regular short rotation. I am glad the chipmunks remained as long as they did for they gave me many a cessation of hoeing corn while I chased them in and out of the crooked worm fences. While trying to circumvent the crows we boys learned that they could not count, for if two persons went into a "blind" and one went out, the crows would come back to the field.

The frost, too, was an enemy to be reckoned with and often injured the corn and the pumpkins. By reason of press of work or of over-moist ground planting might be delayed until the first days of June and replanting to make good the skips, might be done still later, in which case an early frost might produce much soft "hog-corn."

I have said there was a great deal of uninspiring work on the farm; but after burning the brush the most beastly work was hoeing corn. If the grassland was mowed one year and then pastured for one or two years, the timothy and clover "ran out" and the blue grass ran in and formed a terribly tenacious sod. Such fields were planted to corn that intro-tillage might serve to eradicate the "pesky" blue grass. The plowing and fitting of the corn ground was imperfect, for the tools were primitive, and so the blue grass roots which already had a start, outgrew the corn, especially if the weather was cool and moist. Bluegrass, in some localities, is counted an excellent pasture and even a good hay grass, but with us it was a great pest — almost as much so as the Canada thistle. The instruments for intro-tillage did not make much impression on the leathery sod, and so it was customary to hand-hoe corn from three to five times. Oh, but that did, locate the soft, undeveloped muscles of boys! It makes my sides quiver again just to write about it, even while I rejoice that corn is usually raised now by horse-hoe culture without any use whatever of the hand hoe.

The fields in our region were small — from two to eight acres. When I grew up I tried to account for this practice which was almost universal in the United States and Canada. As usual, my mother solved the question for me. Each field represented a year's clearing and it was about as easy to dispose of the timber by splitting it into rails as to log and burn it. If the year's clearing was fenced by itself the grazing livestock would keep down the vigorous growth of sprouts and weeds which were certain to appear after the brush had been burned and even while the new ground summer fallow was being conducted, for not more than half of the cleared ground was plowable the first year on account of roots and stumps.

The farm buildings on our place consisted of a one and a half story house, two barns — when I was in my teens — a wagon-house and a wood-house. The barns, though of good size, were not large enough to hold the entire crop without much tramping of hay and much care in mowing away the grain. One man, on his knees, placed the sheaves in well-arranged parallel rows and by hitching along pressed them down as the line extended; but even so, the grain would settle and the peaks would have to be refilled from the ladder. A modern curb-roof would have eliminated much of the old roof structure, would have nearly doubled the capacity of the mows, saved labor and obviated the pain of picking thistles out of the knees and hands. It is interesting to note that many of the low barns of Central New York built on the old model, are now being enlarged upward and improved by using the curb-roof construction.

I have long since learned that we husked the corn, dug the potatoes, and picked the apples too late in the season, for we and they often suffered from the fall blasts and the approaching winter. There were times when I would have gone the distance of a block out of my way to avoid the sight of one of those jumbo apple trees. Imagine a twenty foot ladder reared against one of those great trees which grew like forest trees because of the store of plant food in the virgin soil, and at the upper end, in that cold northwest wind, a lad with numbed hands grasping the ladder with one hand and the apples with the other — and you

have a true picture of some of my boyhood hardships.

These apples were loaded into a New Jersey
scoop wagon box with side boards; forty or more
bushels of them, and hauled ten miles with three
horses. The span was so hitched to long double-
trees and neck yokes that they straddled one path,
while the lead horse took it, by which arrangement
the wagon wheels ran in the paths followed by the
tongue horses and escaped the all but bottomless
ruts. In the market apples brought eighteen and
three-fourths cents per bushel in "shinplasters,"
redeemable at the store where the prices were
about 100 per cent. above cost.

No one understood then and few understand
now, that the difference between our outgo and
our income was largely secured through parting
with the unearned natural resources of the land,
such as wood, humus, nitrogen, potash and phos-
phate of lime. That is, our profits were not all
due to wise plans, economy and hard work. Even
to this day such misleading, incorrect balance
sheets are being struck in the minds of a multitude
of farmers. And yet in spite of this I am fully
persuaded that a well-informed young man, with
a farm paid for and a little surplus capital, could

now find no better place to raise apples than on that same farm of my boyhood, depleted as it is of some of its plant food; nor perhaps could he find any other business likely to bring more liberal rewards in pleasure and money for the money and the effort expended. What more comfortable place to live in and get joy out of life than on the banks of one of those finger lakes! You may ask: Why did not I or one of my children see all this twenty-five years ago? As for myself my sad experience in those apple trees and my ignorance of fruit culture dampened my ardor and misled my judgment. As for my boys, they, like other young people, imagine that escape from difficulties and hardships awaits them at the other end of the world; distance, too, has a wonderful enchantment:

> " Hope springs eternal in the human breast,
> Man never is, but always to be blest."

I could not blame my children since I myself listened to the " call of the wild " and moved westward three times; if I go farther, I shall land in the east on the other side of the world.

But to return to our difficulties in that early time: plowing was laborious and provoking not only because of the stumps but because the plows were crude, heavy and inefficient. A few wooden moldboards were still in use when I first reached up to those handles which were all too short and too high even for men. Why plow makers persisted for half a century in so wooding the plows as to give the short end of the lever to the plowman and the long one to the horses, I could never understand, unless it was to permit of throwing the plow in behind the stumps quickly as it passed them. There was certainly no excuse for setting the handles so high that they were certain to hit the plowboy in the ribs if the plowshare received a sidethrust. Cast plows superseded those made of wood chiefly, or by the blacksmith of wrought iron, but they were heavy unpolished implements and in many respects violated the principles of plow construction as we now know them. They were hard to hold when going ahead and harder to pull back when they struck their noses under a network of roots. In some respects they were not as good as the more primitive peacock plow, for it was provided with a lock-colter so that it could not get its nose fast under the roots and it was also lighter to handle.

Harrows, or, more accurately, drags, were at first made from the symmetrical crotches of trees and with a dozen wooden teeth. The virgin soil did not need fining but smoothing, for it was mixed with soft leaf mould. But as the stumps rotted away the soil changed in character and the farmer learned to construct iron-toothed harrows that were more efficient. Let me remark here that working farmers were the original inventors of nearly every agricultural implement — and of most of the common tools used on the farm. While the initial idea was often only partially and crudely developed, the inventors should receive due credit. The spade, the shovel, the hoe, the flail and the fan were invented long before iron was available. In like manner the sled, the wagon, the harness, the thresher, the rake, the harvester — all were first invented by the farmer. Necessity was indeed the parent of invention.

GROWING UP

I must now go back a little from the consideration of the social and industrial conditions under which I grew up, to certain apparently unimportant events which were later to shape my life quite differently from the lives of my brothers.

When I was about fifteen years old I went home from school one evening with my cousins, the Burroughs boys. In one part of my uncle's new and as yet unfinished house, I found a middle-aged man from Pennsylvania, by the name of Moyer, working at a bench by candle-light. The long, ribbony shavings had, in the uncertain light, a wonderful charm for me and I determined at once to learn carpentering and asked my uncle if he would hire me to work with Moyer the next summer. I had previously worked for my uncle on the farm at $1.25 per week. My uncle agreed that I was to receive for six months $10 per month and board, and it was stipulated that I was to leave the bench and work in the harvest field at least two weeks of the time as a "half-hand," that is, to bind one-half what a cradler cut. When harvest came, however, uncle put two other half-hands with me to take up after two cradlers. We argued among ourselves as to how three halves could be united so as to make two whole ones; but fortunately workmen had not then learned to strike and the work went on. We had been taught the wise saying of Solomon: "when the ax is dull, lay on the harder."

The money earned by carpentering enabled me that fall to attend the Academy at Seneca Falls and later, as I became more skilled, I earned the money to go on again with my studies. The next year but one my uncle gave me $1 per day to work at repairing buildings on his son's farm. The older children in our family did not have to work so hard as I did to get an education, for they went to school when the household was more prosperous. While I was growing up there were several serious illnesses in the family and there was less money to spend for other purposes. One of these occurred just as I was about ready to go to the Academy, and prevented me from getting any more formal education.

When I was about sixteen or seventeen years old I was possessed with a desire to visit my Grandfather Roberts, then nearly eighty years of age, and the other relatives living near Trenton, New Jersey. After urging the matter upon my mother several times, she finally said: "Child, you know we haven't the money to spare." That seemed to shatter all my hopes; but not long afterward I asked: "Well, may I go if I can earn the money?" And she replied with a smile: "Why, yes, I think so." In the modern slang, it was now "up to me." Immediately I made diligent inquiry for carpenter work; and soon learned that an assembly hall — an extension to a hotel — was to be built in a hurry for a political convention, at a village some five miles away. In ten minutes I was astride of old Nance, and that day I got a job.

I must have worked at least four weeks when my employer asked what wages I thought I ought to have. As I hesitated a good fellow, a half-fledged workman who had worked alongside me, said: "Well, the boy has earned as much as I have." That settled it—I got $1.25 per day and board—very good wages at that time. I can scarcely describe with what pride I came home with the biggest roll of bills I had ever possessed in my pocket; nor my joy in filling the old family carpet-bag with little love tokens, for our unsuspecting relatives in New Jersey. Of all my travelling experiences that first one was the most exciting —probably because it was the first.

But the journey was planned with many misgivings, for up to this time I had seen nothing of the outside world. I had been to Seneca Falls, eleven miles away; and to Ovid, eight miles away; across the Lake to Aurora—four miles—and greatest of all, I had once driven the school teacher to Sodus Bay—thirty miles. Now I was about to take a "truly" journey on the steam cars, into the very crater of what I then supposed was the wickedest city on earth — for hair-raising stories of New York used to come to us by way of the canal, our dock being the terminal of a line of Erie Canal boats. I now realize that if those stories had come by fast mail instead of the " raging canal " they would not have had time to grow so large. Some strange things did happen to me but at this distance of time they appear laughable rather than terrifying.

In that Hades to which I was hastening I knew but one person, a former schoolmate who kept a small fruit store on Broadway. As the train approached the city in the early evening the cars stopped more frequently and passengers began to get off; but was this Broadway? If not, where was it? I hesitated to ask questions for fear they might reveal my country breeding. I finally came to this sage conclusion : the ocean must be here and the cars cannot carry me beyond New York city — but I was fairly quaking with terror. At last the train pulled into a great station, the last, apparently; and as all the remaining passengers arose, I went out also, not knowing whither I went.

Again I reasoned that most of these passengers must live on Broadway and so I trailed after the largest crowd and soon came to a street that was busier and lighter than others, where I began to look for the numbers above the stores. By this time I saw that I was going in the wrong direction, but thinking that someone might observe that I was green, I continued to a cross street, went over and started in the right direction, then walked a block crossing over again to the even-numbered side. After many weary blocks I found the store number of my friend and I do not know whether he was more surprised at the sight of me or at the size of my carpet-bag.

I woke early the next morning, full of curiosity, and conceived the brilliant idea of going out to see the city before breakfast. I thought I took note of the location of the house, but after a time when I turned back the houses seemed all alike and I knew that I was lost. After a time of anxious wandering my friend came out to hunt me and fortunately found me at the corner of the next block. I cannot remember a single thing I saw that October morning but I learned that you cannot see the town for the houses.

When I came back to New York from Hunterdon County my bag was heavily laden with presents and souvenirs for those at home and I had a good, stout cane, a present from my grandfather

4

to my father. I had thought I could find my way but again I got lost and it was nearing train-time. So, seeing a ragged boy scarcely larger than my valise, I exclaimed: "Here, boy, carry my baggage," in a tone such as I imagined a distinguished traveller might use. "Where do you want to go?" he asked. "Oh, to the New York Central depot," I replied. But I had hardly begun to follow him when it occurred to me that the boy — the son of a thief perhaps — might get away with all my treasures; and I planned to lay him low with the family cane. When he finally led me safely to the station, I gave him a quarter with the air of some wealthy up-country farmer. It may appear to you that this is an exaggerated account of a very trivial affair but how serious it was to an ignorant, imaginative boy whose mind had been filled with blood-curdling stories by those lying up-state canalers, is shown by the fact that I now remember it much more distinctly than the city sights which I had come to view.

Arriving safely at home I was the envy of all my school mates and was even looked up to by some of my elders. From the time of this journeying until I was about twenty I carpentered most of the time in summer and spent the winters at the

Academy. When I was twenty-one I was employed, on the reputation of my brothers as good teachers, to teach the winter school at the small village of Beerytown, which with the surrounding countryside, furnished about eighty pupils of school age. The school proved to be well-advanced not only in books but in deviltry and had a large per cent of nearly-grown boys who had made it warm for my predecessor, got him into a law suit and finally succeeded in getting him dismissed. Later I made the acquaintance of this gentleman who became a well-known scholar and who, for many years, was Secretary of State for New York.

I did not have very much difficulty in governing the school but the larger boys and girls kept me screwed up to concert pitch all the time. One young lady kept me hard at work preparing the lessons in Watson's Mental Arithmetic — an old textbook which was, in fact, a mental algebra. A laughable little thing happened in this wise: The boys were requested to bring in some wood on their return from recess. They obeyed quite literally. Every boy loaded his arms to his nose and, marching in Indian file, they deposited such a quantity of stove wood as had never been seen in the school-house at one time. One small boy, after unloading, tarried to see the others come in; as a big boy passed him he tripped and the big boy and the load of wood both went sprawling to the floor. Before the uproar had ceased I had the little fellow by the shoulders of his round-a-bout coat and, with one upward surge, the coat was in my hands and his pants on the floor. "My scat!" that was a scene for an artist! For the boy had no shirt — or perhaps it was inside the coat — I did not stop to investigate — but with a face as red as those of the larger girls, I crushed him to the floor, gathered him and the wreckage in my arms, thrust them together into the basket room, and sent his brother in after him. Soon afterward he appeared, clothed, and I lived for several days in nervous dread of hearing from this ridiculous episode, but nothing happened.

In those days the first thing the older pupils tried to do was to "stick" the teacher. The following will show a few of the ways in which they tried to "stick" me. A boy more than twenty years old called me to his seat and expressed a great desire to master all there was in Thompson's Higher Arithmetic and wished to begin on the first page in Roman notation and to follow with every succeeding process. I helped him through addition and sat up nights to prepare for the difficulties ahead but, fortunately, my ambitious pupil dropped out in a few days. Soon after this, another advanced boy called for help in Algebra. It was an easy job to straighten out his X, Y, Z's; but the next day he wanted help again. When asked if he had performed all the examples between the two widely separated problems — they were thirty pages apart — he said no, that he was just reviewing. He had struck a tough one, as I had reason to remember for I had had it at the Academy. So, glancing at it, I remarked casually: "Jacob, I am too busy to do that long example in school hours." As it was then time for recess I turned the boys out and walked with shaking knees to my desk to get my old algebra. Upon turning over the fly leaves, I found that example all worked out as I had done it in the Academy. Going to the blackboard, I transcribed it, and when the boy came in I said in no uncertain tone: "Jacob, there is your problem!" Not having succeeded in "sticking" me, he soon afterward left school.

The boys tried other tricks than merely intellectual problems. The teacher of the previous winter was accustomed to go to the hotel for his mid-day meal. While he was gone they would bar the door on the inside, thus shutting out the teacher, who would go up the street and return with a school trustee. By the time they reached the schoolhouse the door would be standing open and all the pupils would be playing in the yard at the back. When I was asked by one of the boys what I would do if I were barred out, I replied promptly, that I would batter down that door with a stick of stove wood and then there would be doings inside. By such bold front and by virtue of good fortune I gained a reputation of being able to govern hard schools where better men than I had failed.

From a letter written to me in recent years by a man who visited my school, I extract the following comments:

"Your autobiography is especially interesting to me because I remember so many incidents of your youthful days. Among them is one of the winter you taught school at Beerytown where the pupils ranged from sixty to seventy in number. J. N. B.— and myself, who were then about twelve years old, made you a visit. When the school was out at noon you took us to dinner with you at the hotel where you boarded and one thing that made a deep impression on my mind was the beefsteak they had on the table — such a lot of it, great thick slices — and so much more than I had ever been used to seeing on the table at one time. The boys in school were great big, rough town boys, but you maintained good order and as I look at it now, you must have had considerable executive ability to manage them.   But what impressed me most was when I asked you if you could work all those hard examples in the back of Davis' Arithmetic, you said you could, and it seemed to me that any person who could do that must be a *highly educated* person. Indeed, I have no mean opinion of it yet — at least when I was old enough to do them I felt rather proud of it."

During that winter one other thing happened which had an influence on my after life.   A cousin of mine was to be married so I got a day off at the end of the week and attended the wedding, after which a party was made up to escort the bride and groom wherever they should choose to go.   A half-dozen young couples in as many sleighs, set out and a merry three days it was for most of us. The following Monday morning I got back home, four miles from my school, sleepy, tired and mad!   My girl had showered her smiles on a handsomer man than I at one of the villages where we had stopped, and as my puppy-love had now passed away and as I had spent the earnings of a whole month, I was in a reflective frame of mind.   By the time I had walked the four miles to my school the old saying, "A fool and his money is soon parted" seemed to me true.   Now, I reckon, that the money spent in those three days, chasing after fun and not finding it, if it had been put at interest and left to accumulate till 1914 would have amounted to the no inconsiderable sum of $824.50. However, I got some wisdom out of that foolish expenditure and perhaps that was worth more to me then than the money would be now.

SECTION II

EARLY MANHOOD IN THE MIDDLE WEST

(1854 — 1873)

HOW I CAME TO GO WEST

In the spring of 1854 my first winter of school teaching came to an end. On the evening of the last day a very creditable exhibition of the school's ability to sing and declaim was held in the very hall that I had helped to erect when I was earning money for that dangerous journey which I made to the " Jarsies" (New Jersey). I was, therefore, out of a job. Why my uncle did not go on adding to his house — it was already 110 feet long — so as to give me employment I did not then quite understand, for I looked upon that vigorous, money-making uncle as a great man who when he got started in a big thing never stopped. Mr. Moyer, the boss-carpenter with whom I had worked at uncle's, had gone to La Porte, Indiana, and there was not much building going on in our neighborhood. I was not needed at home on the farm and there was, in short, no work in sight.

Perhaps I was still a little sore over the month's wages squandered in that joy-ride of the previous winter; at any rate I was restless and unhappy. I could no longer lie on the grass on the lake bank and dream, for I was now a man in the eyes of the law and felt that I must be getting a foothold in the world. One Sunday I heard that there was a contractor visiting a neighbor about half a mile down the Lake and I determined to interview him; but having also heard that he was a hard boss I loitered and debated whether I really wanted a job under him. Just as I came in sight of the neighbor's house I saw the man I had come to see drive away.

But that proved to be a piece of good fortune for soon afterward I received a letter from Moyer, my old boss, offering me a dollar and a quarter a day and board in Indiana. So I quickly packed all my belongings including my tools, in one trunk, and turning my back on old Cayuga's waters, I travelled westward with the "Star of Empire" to La Porte. I still have a vivid recollection of arriving before daylight in that prairie town whose only pavement was sticky mud, on a foggy morning in April. It was not a grown-up man but a tired, sleepy, hungry boy who found his way to the hotel.

Did *you* ever arrive at one of those dirty country hotels while every joint was aching from a night's wrestle with a jump-car seat, only to meet a surly porter already half asleep? I must confess that that morning was one of the gloomiest in my life.

From the banks of picturesque Cayuga, from a clean home and loving friends; to these muddy ague-breeding prairie streets, this filthy hotel and these unfriendly faces, was all to sudden-like.

But when I had had a good wash-up and breakfast, and when the fog had lifted, my new-found country looked more attractive though it seemed far too flat to my unaccustomed eyes. A walk of about a mile brought me to the house of a Mr. Allen where I found my old boss, Moyer, at work with his white shirt-sleeves rolled up and his bright red undershirt flaming among the white shavings. The long ribbons that he sliced off the side of a board were as beautiful to me in my homesickness as those that had charmed me and given direction to my life long before in my uncle's unfinished house. By 1 o'clock of the same day I was working on the other side of the bench from that patient, kind and expert Pennsylvanian.

The cornice — which we were preparing by hand, millwork then being unknown — was for a house to be erected on one of Mr. Allen's farms three miles away. One morning a gang of well diggers passed on their way to sink a well on this farm; upon seeing them returning about sun-down of the same day I remarked that something must be wrong. Mr. Allen explained that doubtless the well was completed, as they were bringing their windlass with them, and I wondered what kind of a well two men could dig in a day! Later, I found out that the well was only fifteen feet deep with four feet of water in it; the soil was porous at the surface, with a layer of sand lower down which began to fill with water at a depth of twelve feet. Even at a depth of six to seven feet there was danger of cave-ins and therefore the well was curbed in the following manner.

A ring perhaps thirty inches inside diameter and four inches wide on its face, was made out of two layers of one inch boards nailed together. Upon this ring when placed in the well, were laid well-bricks — about fourteen to the circle — until the surface of the ground was reached. The digging could then go on safely and, as the sand was removed, the brick wall settled and more bricks were added at the top. As soon as the water began to come in the sand was scooped out with a curious dipper which had its handle attached at an acute angle. When the water rose to the arm-pits of the digger, or rather, when the digger sank into the water by reason of the removal of the quicksand, the well was considered finished. If the water ever became too shallow, more quicksand was removed, permitting the wall of the well to settle and more bricks to be added at the top. On several occasions afterwards the knowledge of this safe method of sinking a well in treacherous earth was most useful to me.

It took us nearly all summer to erect Mr. Allen's house and repair the barn and while the latter was in progress I had my first experience with fever and ague. In those days Peruvian bark and whiskey bitters, quinine and blue-mass pills, were the invariable remedies or, more accurately speaking, palliatives, for when cold weather came on the disease disappeared only to return the following year.

In the fall we got a job to build a house on Hog Prairie, the very name of which implied still more unhealthy conditions. Colonel Place, Ex-Mayor of La Porte, owned a large tract of land along the sluggish, meandering Kankakee river, upon which cattle were grazed. One of his neighbors said it was a rich farm but there were two objections to it: six months in the year cattle had to be driven three miles to the river to get a drink, and the other six months they had to be loaded on a flat-boat in order to have safe standing ground while they drank.

One day, after we had been driven thirty miles across country in a two-horse lumber wagon, we began framing the house which was to take the place of a log shanty. The old shanty, which was still occupied by a family, was built of poles rather than logs, about sixteen by eighteen feet in length and was low at the eaves; a " grecian-bend " doorway and a floor of wide, unmatched boards rested directly on the wet ground. Sometime before our arrival the chimney and the fire-place had fallen down leaving a hole about five by six feet in the side of the house which was covered with something resembling a blanket. One day at dinner we were much startled by a squeal "too dread for any earthly throat:" the pot of hot, boiled potatoes had been set aside and a hog had slipped inside behind this curtain and sampled them.

Between the low door and the stove there was a low pile of corncobs which served for fuel in the day-time and as a warm lounging place in the evening for the smaller children. The proverbial latchstring had long since vanished and the latch with it; an angling auger hole for receiving a pin had been bored into the end of one of the door logs and whenever anyone wished to enter someone on the inside had to unloose the pin. Some of the boys substituted a corn cob for the wooden pin and then when there was a quick push on the door the cob would break and the door come open. A fresh cob served to secure the door again and to push the broken one out.

The first evening I wondered where we were all to find lodgment for there were in the family a father and mother, two grown daughters, a big boy, a man boarder and four younger lads, besides Moyer and myself. It reminded me of the land-lord's puzzle which was current in my boyhood: the problem was to put seven men in six beds, having only one in a bed and yet all in bed at the same time. The solution of our problem was how-ever, much more pressing — it was how to put twelve persons comfortably to sleep in four visible beds. It was not until later that I discovered how it was attempted. The parents and one of the smaller children slept in the kitchen bed, the two grown girls in an invisible one under it. The big son and the boarder slept in the second bed; three of the kids in the third; and we two carpenters in the fourth — all three of these being in the Lean-to which was only about ten feet wide and sixteen feet long. There was a small piece of glass left in the sash to mark where a window had been and when you entered the Lean-to you might stand erect but as you advanced you had to " jouk."

I do not know how successful the Colonel was with cattle on Hog Prairie, but we had auricular demonstration of the success of cat multiplication. After seven of us had snuggled down in that sunken Lean-to the cats would begin to land on the floor by twos and threes — with feline instinct they came through the paneless window to find a soft warm place on our beds. If they became too obstreperous someone would declare war and then there was a regular blue streak of cats, as the boys would say.

There comes back to me an appropriate verse from a parody on the " Ode to Music " which I learned in my boyhood and often declaimed from the stage:

" Then came a boy loud whooping to the gale,
    And on his truant shoulders bore a pole;
Two furious cats, suspended by the tail,
    Were swinging cheek by jowl.
O dulcet cats, what was your delighted measure
With claws deep buried in each other's face?
How did ye hiss and spit your venom round
With murderous yells of more than earthly sound.
O dulcet cats! Could one more pair like you
The concert join and pour the strain anew,
Not man could bear nor demons ear sustain
The fiendish caterwaul of rage and pain."

Time fails to tell of all the other living things there were in that lean-to besides men and boys and cats, but I must not forget to say that the family did everything it was in their power to do under the circumstances to make us comfortable.

Close by the house a railway ran along an unfenced right of way and one day the cowcatcher caught a steer — one of the Colonel's fattest — and pitched it into the ditch. For a month thereafter we feasted on beef, the weather being cool, and with plenty of other food fairly well cooked, we had nothing to complain of except those filthy sleeping quarters and the vermin that bunked with us. As the two girls were fairly proficient on the violin and the boys could sing a little, the evenings were spent not altogether unpleasantly, so long as we took no thought of the night. I have already taken so much time in describing the surroundings and the first part of our stay in that land of flatness, mosquitoes and ague, that I will have to pass over certain unique local characters and hasten on with my story.

As might have been expected the ague returned upon me and after battling with it for a few days I boarded the cars on a Saturday morning and went to Salem Junction where I expected to get a train for La Porte. But unfortunately, the only train by which I could reach La Porte before midnight had already passed and I was obliged to stay there. A raging fever and a bed already occupied by one or two specious of indigenous fauna were not conducive to sleep. The next day I found a sunny place in a little wood adjoining where I did get a few fitful naps and at last, on Monday morning, having virtually neither slept nor eaten for thirty-eight hours, I reached La Porte in a desperate state! By accident I met Colonel Place's wife at the station and when she saw how sick I was she insisted that I must go home with her and be cared for. I felt hardly fit to sleep in a stable and the thought of contaminating one of her immaculate beds was worse even than the ague, but she compelled me to yield. In about two weeks I returned to Hog Prairie and remained well until the house was completed.

That first fall in Indiana was a severe test of my courage and endurance. I was often tempted to go back to the old home in New York where I would have been most warmly welcomed but I am thankful that I did not go for the fates were kinder the longer I stayed. Somehow it seems to do boys good to pitch them out of the home nest when they are young and let them get used to turning short corners while they are supple.

I engaged rooms and board for the winter in the house which we had erected on Stillwell prairie, as building could not go on in winter and I did not expect to have work.   Mr. Armstrong, with whom I was stopping, had two nearly grown boys and was anxious about their winter schooling, for it had been decided that the old school house was un-inhabitable.   Finding out that I had taught school in New York, and that I was ready to do almost anything to avoid an idle winter, it was agreed that I was to teach in the condemned school house ex-cept during the extreme cold days.   A dollar per day and board was certainly small wages, but better than a winter's board bill and the blues.

On the coldest days only the larger pupils would put in an appearance.   The window cracks were corked with paper and the loose benches arranged in a hollow square around the stove for the pupils while I, with overcoat on, walked around the out-side of the square and gave help and heard recita-tions.   By noon the stove would be so full of un-consumed coals from too rapid firing that they had to be carried out and a new fire built.   I wonder now that we did not set that old red school house afire by our reckless stoking.

Nothing worth relating happened that winter except, perhaps, the following little incident. One morning I said to my host: "I am certain to have chills and fever today, and when the fever is at its height I am often flighty — I don't want to make a fool of myself — but I don't like to dismiss school."

"Go to the cupboard and take a good swig from that jug of whiskey-and-Peruvian bark bitters," said he. I did as directed, ate a little breakfast and upon attempting to rise from the table remarked: "Armstrong, I'm drunk!"

"Oh, that's nothing," said he, "you took it on an empty stomach. Take another good big swig to sober yourself and then run all the way to the school house!"

Since I was taking the Armstrong treatment, I obeyed. The snow was about a foot deep and the horses and sleigh runners had formed two narrow slippery paths. Such paths are hard enough to walk in when sober, and for a man light in the head it was an impossible task. So I essayed a dog-trot, leaving many footprints outside the beaten track; but I arrived at the school house sober as he had predicted and I had no delirium that day.

As soon as the school closed in the spring Moyer and Roberts formed a verbal copartnership and employed one journeyman and two apprentices. Moyer was to receive $2 and I $1.50 per day and board. We also received twenty-five cents a day out of the wages of each of the others for the use of the tools, et cetera, with which we furnished them. We usually began work immediately after an early breakfast and worked until sundown, with an hour's nooning and the time to eat a 5 o'clock supper, taken out — making a twelve-hour day.

The second winter I taught the Stillwell school and received $1.25 per day and boarded round. The school had become demoralized because of teachers who were deficient in ability to control large boys. Firm but just treatment and a few osage-orange switches, carried me and the pupils through safely. The larger boys got into the habit of playing "fox and hounds" which resulted in their not being present sometimes when the afternoon session began. I requested them not to go beyond the sound of the school bell; they soon broke this rule and one day they found the school door locked against them. When they had all arrived I opened it and marched them all in and stood them around the hot stove to dry. One of the other pupils was sent to the osage-orange fence and directed to cut and bring me eight whips. Meanwhile I had taken so much time to consider the matter that standing around the hot stove became a punishment. I knew that it was a dangerous situation for, in the previous winter, the large pupils had placed the teacher in one of the seats and then a pupil had gone through the motions of teaching the school.

In order to get the advantage of them I arranged the eight in a row and taking one of the whips — which were quite brittle — I gave the first boy one good cut and commanded him in no uncertain tone: "Take your seat!" The second boy was served with switch number two and the same command, and so on down the line. Before the job was half done someone laughed, then all of them roared, even the lads who were receiving one stroke each, and what was a dangerous beginning ended happily on both sides. The news of this affair spread through the countryside and I gained a reputation for clever discipline and very cheaply withal.

In changing from teaching to carpentering in the spring and *vice versa* in the fall I rarely lost

Margaret Marr Roberts
(Mrs. I. P. Roberts) 1887.

more than a day's work. The following summer
Moyer and I added two more hands to our building gang; this gave him twenty-one shillings per
day — $2.62½ — and me seventeen shillings —
$2.12½ — and our board. Since we always did
country carpentering, expenses were almost a neg-
ligible quantity: clothing, Sunday board and washing altogether, only slightly reduced my savings. I
had learned my lesson long before when taking
that joy-ride while I was teaching at Beerytown.

At the end of three years of alternate teaching
and carpentering, on the 3d day of November,
1857, I was married to Margaret Jane Marr,
daughter of William and Mary (Reader) Marr
who had moved about ten years previously from
Pennsylvania to a farm near La Porte, Indiana.
Mr. Marr was of direct Scotch origin and Mrs.
Marr of German and Dutch ancestry.

My wife and I left immediately for a trip to
my old home in New York. The journey was accomplished with difficulty in those days for the
country was flooded with wild-cat paper money
which would not pass outside of the state in which
it was issued, and gold exchange could not be secured at any discount. Although I had sufficient
wild-cat money brought from Indiana, I had to

borrow money from a brother for the return journey. By the first of December I was back in the Stillwell school house and again teaching. In the spring of 1858 on taking stock of my resources three years after my arrival in Indiana, I found that I had about $700 loaned out at 10 per cent. interest, $100 in bills receivable, and a most charming wife — value as yet unknown.

That same spring I purchased forty-eight acres of land on the edge of the little village of Kingsbury; moved into some upper rooms there and began to build a modest one-and-a-half story house. My brother-in-law, Daniel Marr, worked the farm while I spent the summer building for myself and others. The following winter I again taught the Stillwell school, boarding at home and walking most of the time a distance of eight miles daily to and from my school. In the spring of 1859 we took an orphan boy about fifteen years of age into the family, who worked on the farm in summer and attended school in winter. This permitted me to spend four or five days of each week away from home, carpentering. I frequently spent Saturday helping the boy catch up with pressing farm work, sometimes doing two days' work in one, as the saying is, which made it pleasant to rest on Sunday.

The following winter I taught the village school, and, for fear I should lack for exercise, I became the sexton of the church.

The farm had been bought just before the prices of farm products had begun to fall — due in part to unrest over the slavery question, and in part to over-production of the leading staples. The monetary conditions — especially in the west, were most unsatisfactory. Money received one day at 100 cents on the dollar, was worth on the next perhaps 80 cents and the following week may be nothing. It did not take a prophet to foresee that the unrest of the country meant trouble, but just how or when the storm would break no one was wise enough to predict. Party lines were being drawn tighter and tighter and the names, " Black Abolitionist " and " Copperhead " began to be bandied about — old friends and even brothers ranging themselves in antagonism.

In spite of these unfortunate conditions I managed to sell the farm in 1862 for as much as I gave for it though I lost most of the value of the improvements. But it had never brought an income sufficient to pay running expenses, if the improvements, such as buildings, fences and added productivity of the land were counted, as they should be. I had spent three years of my life in faithful work, chiefly carpentering, without much financial advancement and, worst of all, I had gained no valuable experience. All the farmers of that time were in a similar case — we were raising products which could not be sold for what it cost to produce them, sometimes not even for one-half.

The last school I taught in Indiana during the winter of 1860–61, was in the new schoolhouse that had supplanted the old one where I first taught. A Democrat withdrew his children from the school because I taught that our government was not a pure democracy but a representative democracy and because, worst of all, I had called our country " a republic." During the following summer I found some work at carpentering but all industrial conditions were growing steadily worse because of the War which had meantime begun.

By this time the firm of Moyer and Roberts had dissolved and the efficient journeymen whom they had employed were scattered — gone west, as most people do when they meet with problems that they cannot solve. We are all very much alike when life grows difficult: instead of fighting it out we are apt to conclude that any change would be for the better and, usually, it is a wise conclusion. The advice given to an old farmer whose pigs were doing badly: "If they are shut up, turn them out, if they are running out, shut them up," was wise if not altogether scientific.

In the winter of 1861–2 for the first time I did not teach school; everything conspired to drive me back to farming. I spent the first part of the winter in pricing land, but it had not gone down with the prices of farm products. Coming home one evening cold, wet and discouraged, I said to my wife: "Let's go west — there is nothing in this country for us!" "I am ready and have been for a year," she replied. "But I'm in earnest," said I. "So am I," she answered promptly and so that momentous decision was made.

Only ten days after this conversation all except a few personal things were sold at public vendue. The two-horse wagon was "bowed" and the ribs first covered with carpeting, and then with oilcloth securely fastened. A thousand pounds, perhaps, of goods which had been packed in boxes, constituted the load. A spring wagon seat, a plank foot-warmer, and plenty of robes and blankets, gave promise of comfort on our long journey. About the middle of February, 1862, two stout horses were in-spanned, and we turned our faces toward Mount Pleasant, Iowa. We chose this place rather than another because Nathan Palmer of Stillwell Prairie, whose children had been in school with me, was living there. If on our overland journey the cold prairie winds should make it too uncomfortable for the mother and baby Mary — then sixteen months old — I planned to send them on ahead by rail, for our route lay nearly parallel with a main line. If it thawed out and if the bottom of the prairie roads fell out as they sometimes did even in mid-winter, the boxes of goods could be shipped and the span and wagon could still be driven to their destination.

As it happened however, the roads were ideal; an early warm spell followed by rain and a sudden freeze had left them hard, smooth and icy; one could almost have skated across the state of Illinois. We always began each day's journey late in the morning, drove rapidly, made the lunch hour short, and put up for the night as early as possible. With the good roads and a team always fresh, although the load exceeded half-a-ton weight, the horses could be kept at a trot most of the time. My horses proved the economy of an eight-hour day. We took the main emigrant road, leading always westward, which was already settled somewhat along its borders; and as the farmers were accustomed and glad to entertain travellers we had little difficulty in obtaining accommodations.

On the 4th day of March, 1862, about 4 p. m., we drove across the Mississippi river, at Burlington, on the ice. We were then only one long day's drive from our destination so instead of stopping in Burlington we pushed on for another hour. For the first time we were turned away from the farmhouses not once but several times, although it had begun to snow and the wind was rising to a gale. By this time the baby was crying from long confinement and cold, so at the next house, we did not even ask for shelter but bundled out and insisted upon being taken in.   In the dark we had not seen that it was a tavern but it proved to be a delightful one; and the next day, a little after noon, we arrived at Mount Pleasant, Iowa, and were among friends.   Notwithstanding the predictions of our friends in Indiana it had been a very comfortable journey; and an instructive one also, although I did not fully digest all the ideas I picked up until afterward.

In a few days I rented forty acres of land adjoining the town limits of Mount Pleasant, which was offered to me a few months later at $35 an acre, including a fairly good house and a small barn — but I did not buy it. Six years afterward I offered $100 an acre for this same land but could not secure it at that price. Taking into consideration the price of farm products at the two periods, the latter price was cheaper than the former. To illustrate the paralysis of business and the poverty of the farmers of the Middle West from 1860 to 1864, some of the prices of farm products may be cited. Soon after my arrival in 1862, a farmer sold me good butter at four pounds for twenty-five cents; seed oats cost me twelve and one-half cents per bushel which was two and one-half cents above the market price; I purchased two two-year-old heifers nearly ready to freshen for $8 a piece, one of which I sold a few years later for $35. Although I was paid in greenbacks, which were variable in value, I was satisfied, since we had gained the use of a good cow for several years.

And this reminds me of one of the little incidents of our emigrant journey. On a Saturday night we stopped at a quiet farmhouse and stayed until Monday morning; on asking for my bill my host replied: " Since you have respected the

Sabbath day I will charge you but half price —
one dollar." For some time I had been carrying
one of those foolish but precious little one-dollar
gold pieces —" good for the eyes," we used to call
them — and I gave him that cherished coin, remarking: "You have been so liberal I will pay
you in real money, not in promises." Ten meals
and horse-feed for a day and two-thirds, for one
dollar in gold, which was equivalent to two dollars
in currency, was certainly liberal. Only yesterday
in this year of 1910 a carpenter worked six hours
for me and charged for a full day, for which I
paid him $5 in gold. From this one might almost
conclude that I made a mistake when I exchanged
the saw and the hammer for the cap and gown.

At the time I settled near Mount Pleasant, Iowa,
the condition of the farmers was most unfortunate;
although in the midst of plenty they were really
very poor. Little hamlets were strung over
those fertile prairies along the railway like tiny
beads on a string. The village was usually on
one side of the track and corn cribs without number on the other side. You might suppose that I
would glory in those ample graneries filled to overflowing with the golden harvest, the result of making a thousand bushels of corn grow where only

5

one buffalo grew before; but did you ever realize what it means to a farmer to sell a bushel — 70 to 75 pounds — of corn in the ear for ten cents? Imagine him if you can, housed in a little, poorly-built pre-emption shanty, eight or more miles from a railway station on a treeless prairie and far from neighbors; and in a climate windy and cold for six months in the year; having always more corn in the field than he can husk and no money with which to purchase the most indispensable things or to employ help to gather in the fall harvest! Imagine, I say, such a farmer, out in the field by sunrise some frosty morning, with a span of horses and wagon, husking a load of corn, which means thirty bushels, and which would keep him at work all of the short autumn day. The next day he must take the corn to one of those long fence-board cribs at the station, ranged parallel with the railroad track — another day's work! And for all this labor of man and team — growing, harvesting and delivery — he received only three paper dollars!

With these he crossed over to the store and traded the value of thirty bushels of corn for clothing for his wife and children and a few indispensable groceries. Is it any wonder that on his return home, after caring for the livestock and milking the cow before he seated himself at the family board — groaning with plenty — he spitefully threw a liberal supply of corn on the fire and said: "Damn you, burn, You ain't worth anything at the station or anywhere else, so I'll keep warm until I enlist and then I suppose the Johnnies will make it warm enough for me without burning corn!"

Those who now occupy those fertile prairies, dotted with groves and orchards amid which are comfortable, well-provisioned homes, can hardly realize the heroism and suffering incident to the settlement of that part of the Middle West which was reclaimed between 1850 and 1863. Production had so far outrun consumption and population as to make many farm products unsalable at any price. No one appeared to understand the trouble much less offered a remedy for it. The struggle for a home on the prairies was, I can but think, a far more severe one than that which had been waged by my ancestors in the wooded districts of Central New York at the beginning of the Nineteenth Century.

The corn cribbed at the station was not shipped for many months after it was produced but was held for speculative purposes. The owners sold it many times but as it could not be stored in Chicago the difference in price between the first day of the month and the last, was paid when the corn was resold. If a part of the corn was really wanted in Chicago it could be shelled and delivered in less than a week. By the end of harvest in 1864 corn had advanced to twenty cents per bushel; at the present time the papers are quoting corn in Chicago at sixty-five cents which price gives the most successful raiser of it possibly ten to fifteen cents per bushel, on the average, clear profit. I had left some cribs of corn in Indiana which I ordered shelled and marketed in the fall of 1863; the returns gave me eighteen cents per bushel net, while it had cost me between thirty and fifty cents to raise that corn!

In the fall of that year I had about thirty acres of corn ready to harvest from the rented forty acres near Mount Pleasant, Iowa. If you ask why I raised corn, my answer is: because everybody else did and because of all farm crops in that region it was the surest, the most easily raised and harvested. A farmer without capital and without harvesting implements was compelled to take the direction of least resistance. I suppose I must

have had between 800 and 1,000 bushels of shelled
corn, that is, 1,200 to 1,500 half bushels of ears,
one and a half bushels of which were counted a
bushel of shelled corn.   It would sell for twenty
cents a bushel, but I had no liking for the job of
husking and marketing thirty acres of corn at that
price.   Fortunately, I had a little money in bank
which I invested in some hogs, thin in flesh, weigh-
ing from 75 to 100 pounds each, at less than two
cents per pound live weight.   The hogs were gathered in a large yard on the borders of a creek and
were fed snapped corn.   It's play to feed snapped
corn with gloves on on a frosty morning and much
more fun to watch the hogs husk it than to husk it
yourself.   I received for the hogs when fat two
cents per pound live weight — no shrinkage —
and through them a trifle over forty centy a bushel
for the corn fed to them, as nearly as I could
estimate it.

I had been told by my father that a bushel of
corn when fed would produce ten pounds of pork
plus enough to pay liberally for the work of feeding it out and caring for the animals.   I had
learned by experience that the most profitable
swine to feed were lean ones — frames, we called
them — which were from six months to one year

of age. I wondered at the time why the owners of the hogs that I purchased, did not feed them to fattening, for even if they had no corn they could make more profit by holding the hogs and buying corn to feed, than by selling them to me. I have since discovered that thoughtless farmers sometimes imagine that by selling both the livestock and the feed they make double money. During that winter I also learned, to my loss, that mature fat cattle can be made to gain very little if any on dry feed, in the winter months, however carefully they may be fed. I have set down the above results in fattening animals to show how I received a valuable part of my education in agriculture.

About one year after we arrived in Mount Pleasant a mild form of varioloid appeared in the town; so mild that few precautions were taken to check its spread. At that time physicians differed widely as to the nature of the disease. Mrs. Roberts, having been exposed to contagion at a public gathering, had a mild case; but my little daughter, Mary, had a severe attack of real small-pox. When the family had about recovered I took an orphan boy about fourteen years of age to raise and to school. Although he had been vaccinated before he came to the house, we had but little faith

in it for we had all been vaccinated and I alone had
escaped — probably owing to a vaccination in my
boyhood.   Therefore when the boy's fever rose
from vaccination we decided at once to move out
to the farm which we had recently purchased and
which was five miles from town.

The farm, or rather the two farms, were in
bad condition and the houses were even worse.
They had been so much neglected that they were
hardly habitable, but we moved in to one of them
and suffered the inconvenience of repairing it over
our heads.   What with these discomforts and
another possible case of small-pox, the first days at
the farm were anything but joyous.   Nor was this
all: an Irish family had come from Indiana expecting to occupy one of the houses and to work a part
of the land.   Their household goods being delayed
in transit, they were allowed to remain in the
house from which we had moved and to use some
of our household fixtures — and they also developed small-pox.   The parents and the oldest
girl had had the disease in Ireland but in just nine
days one of their children came down and in eighteen days, another.

I brought to the farm some mother hogs and
their offspring; by mid-summer they had all died

with the hog cholera, save two or three that recovered but might better have died. Before I could start raising hogs again the farm had to be disinfected or at any rate, all the places where the hogs had ever nested. There was no barn or stable on the place and the cattle of the former owner had spent most of the time during the previous winter on the leeward side of the house, consequently our dwelling was surrounded by a muddy, poached barnyard without fences.

That spring was, however, the darkness that comes just before daylight. I had paid out all my money on the farms and was still in debt; I could not buy hogs so I sowed a large area to oats which, fortunately, sold for fifty cents per bushel. I used to haul 100 bushels to the load, that is, I received fifty dollars as compared to the three dollars per load which the Illinois farmers had received for their corn two years previously. The next summer, however, my hold-over snap corn sold at the crib for seventy cents per bushel.

I think it was in January, 1864, that my wife and I took stock again and found that we were out of debt and that the farm was paid for. Sometime during the latter part of that month we left home on a Saturday to attend some meetings at

the Baptist Church in Mount Pleasant, expecting
to return on Monday.   On coming out of the
church after the Saturday evening service we were
met by Patrick, our tenant, and told that our
house and all its contents had been burned up.
There was no insurance — the house was hardly
worth insuring — but we had hoped it would serve
until a new one could be built.

How did it get on fire?   That will never be
known.   Bridget, the wife of Patrick, was what
we called " a rank Copperhead," and I had given
her great offense by hiring two colored boys who
had drifted over the Missouri line into Iowa.   On
the night of the fire Bridget's son by a former marriage, a deserter from the army and said to be a
professional bounty jumper, was at home.   On
this night they had on tap a jug of whiskey and
had held high carnival, Bridget as usual taking the
lead.   On the following Monday a neighbor
brought us some cooking utensils which had been
found in a fence corner near Bridget's house.
When questioned, Bridget said that she had
rushed into the burning house and got them and
being frightened, had left them by the fence.   But
the neighbors who first arrived at the fire reported
that no one was able to go farther than into the

woodhouse.   From these particulars you are able
to judge as well as I, how our house took fire.

It was indeed a sorrowful Sunday when I went
out to view the ruins; but on my way back to town
on Monday, Mr. O. H. P. Buchanan, a neighbor,
hailed me and handed me a check for one hundred
dollars, saying: "Take this, there will be no interest on it and do not return it until it will not inconvenience you in the least to do so.   Don't run
in debt but pay cash even if you have to borrow at
ten per cent interest!"   That advice was, I think,
worth another hundred dollars.   But that sum did
not go far when bed-ticking and coarse muslin
ranged from sixty to eighty cents per yard and
other household things in proportion, so I bor-
rowed another hundred from another friend.   On
Tuesday we returned to the farm with a wagon-
load of goods and moved into a large room in a
kindly neighbor's house, not far from the site of
our own.

By this time we had a warm place in our hearts
for friends and neighbors without regard to their
politics or faith.   Before leaving town I stepped
into a store to purchase a Bible and, while selecting
one, the fire was discussed.   As the book was being
wrapped up a stranger reached over my shoulder

and laid the price of it on the counter. I learned afterwards that this man was a livestock buyer who on occasion made the air blue with profanity when the cattle and hogs which were being driven to the cars were not of his way of thinking.

As soon as possible the rent house which Patrick had lived in at the other side of the farm was moved, by means of two long skids and eight span of oxen and horses, and placed over the ashes of the one which had been burned. Now it is no easy life to remodel an old house and put a half story on top of it while living in it and at the same time to work as I did, most of the time, ten hours per day on the farm. That summer I worked fully fourteen hours per day and occasionally sixteen hours when I put on lath by candle light.

You may wonder what we ate and drank — I say we, for the wife worked as hard as I did—that we were able to endure such toil. Well, we did not breakfast on cornflakes or wheat germs nor drink Java or Mocha, for it would have taken, at one time, five bushels of corn to buy one pound of coffee. The beverage we drank was made of roasted sorghum; that is, scorched home-made molasses which had enough of a bitter taste to make you think it was just going to taste like coffee; or sometimes, from roasted corn, rye, wheat or sweet potatoes. When you became tired of one you were not compelled to use it for there were half a dozen others to choose from. We drank of that " war coffee " and tried to believe it was good; and I trust we have been forgiven for that self-deception. But even after these long years, my stomach rises up in rebellion at so much as the smell of " postum " or chicory — give me the drink that cheers but does not inebriate the soldier on his long marches! We had almost no fruit and lived chiefly on the staple foods raised on the farm. If one has two good cows, as we had, they may be made to furnish one-half of a good living; and a loving wife, if stress comes, will usually manage the other half.

Many years before this time when quite a small lad, I had set in the front yard of the old New York homestead, with the assistance of my mother, a black cherry tree. When I revisited the old home with my bride I had cut our initials in its bark; now in the fall after we were burnt out there came with other things from home, a half bushel of dried cherries from that tree. Thus dried they appeared to be about nine-tenths pit;

but when stewed they made an appetizing dish and perhaps tasted better for having come from a tree that had been thrice sanctified.

By the time we got fully settled in the re-modelled house we were a thousand dollars in debt. Not having much corn to husk that first year — having raised oats largely — I engaged to build a small house for a neighbor and during the winter I taught my last public school.   All this was an effort to get out of sight of the poorhouse, for in my young days I had visited a county almshouse nearly as bad as the one described in Eggleston's *Hoosier Schoolmaster* and it had made a profound impression on my mind. Up to that time I had had no very definite plan of life but for a while after-ward my chief effort was to make tracks away from that horror of my boyhood; and the diffi-culties I encountered compelled me to think to a purpose and to make farther-reaching plans.

Without attempting to set down exactly the dates of the incidents of the six or seven years I spent here, I may relate some of the more import-ant of them.   Not long after I moved out to this farm, Mr. O. H. P. Buchanan induced me to take 150 of his fine-wool ewes on shares — I to feed and care for them and to deliver to him one-half of the washed wool and one-half of the lambs.   I

bought some sheep on my own account also and
what with these and the increase, I soon had a
flock of about five hundred. So many animals, of
course, could not be pastured on eighty acres of
arable and twenty acres of rough pasture land and
still leave sufficient area for growing forage. To
the north of the emigrant road near which we
lived, there was a vast tract of prairie land as yet
unoccupied. Five of us farmers joined our flocks
into a band of more than three thousand, and employed a Scotch shepherd to herd them there day
and night, someone going out with provisions to
him once a week. This left our farm land free
for raising corn and hay. The corn was cut and
stooked (shocked) in the field; in the winter it was
drawn as wanted and after it was widely spread,
the sheep husked and shelled it, saving us thereby
much disagreeable work. It will be observed that
a portion of our profits were due to "smouching"
the natural resources of the unoccupied prairie
lands, but it is the custom and the common law as
well, that perishable products on uninclosed land
may be used by anyone, provided no notice for-
bidding it has been posted.

Through the sheep land ran a sluggish but clear
creek in which the sheep were washed in the following manner: A chute, wide enough for one

sheep at a time to pass down it, was set with one end in the stream the other against the steep bank at an angle of about forty-five degrees. On the bank a bottle-shaped corral was built, the neck of the bottle opening into the head of the chute and the enclosure being large enough to accommodate the entire band. Next, a lane of two fences was constructed in the creek, of stakes and one board, one end opening at the lower end of the chute and the other on the opposite bank well up stream.

On some fine morning the owners of the sheep and their wives and children, with well-filled picnic baskets, hied them to the washing place where the sheep were already corralled. A man at the head of the chute grasped a sheep by the nape of the neck and sent it down this slippery, narrow way. Since the sheep could not come back nor stand still, it made a virtue of necessity and took a merry skate down the toboggan slide. When it reached the stream, another man, by means of a forked pole, baptized each sheep as it entered the lane and turned it up-stream. It was fun to sit on the bank and see the ancient saw: " One go, all go sheep," verified; and when they were all run through once we ate our picnic dinner while they were soaking. During the afternoon the sheep were compelled to take another plunge and the so-called washing was complete. I have never heard of this mode of washing sheep being practiced anywhere else except in Henry County, Iowa.

After washing the sheep were allowed to run for two or three weeks that the yolk might be restored to the wool and pliancy of fibre and additional weight secured. Then they were brought in to one of the farms, shorn, and the wool banked up in the wool room. About eighteen to twenty thousand pounds were in the storage pile and finally sold to a Boston wool merchant for ninety-seven cents per pound. For rams' fleeces, unwashed, one-half was deducted; if washed, one-third, and for pulled wool the same reduction was made. That was certainly a good price for wool, poorly washed as it was.

I sacked and delivered my share of the wool at one load and banked a little over $1,700. Best of all, perhaps, I sold soon after all my sheep though not before the price had greatly depreciated. I sold because I was afraid that history was about to repeat itself, and it did. I had read in Randall's "Practical Shepherd" that Mr. Livingston — once American Minister to France — had sold in 1810 his unwashed wool from his pure-bred

Spanish Merinos for two dollars a pound and that during the war of 1812 wool rose to two-fifty per pound. At that time the best of imported rams sold for a thousand dollars apiece and a few ewes were sold for like sums. But in 1815 the Peace of Ghent was concluded and within a year thereafter full-blooded Merinos were sold as low as one dollar per head.

To illustrate some of the uncertainties that beset sheep-raising at this period I jot down the experience of one of my neighbors. He had a flock of nice, " straight " two-year-old ewes, for which he was offered twenty-five dollars a head. But they had been in a field where it was possible they might have picked up the germs of footrot; and as he did not like to face possible damages for selling infected animals and did not think it wise to reveal the fact that the flock had grazed on pasture which had once been contaminated, he declined to sell. The sheep remained sound so far as footrot was concerned but unfortunately they later contracted the scab — a skin disease due to a minute insect, the *icarus* — and two years after he received this offer, most of this flock of ewes had to be slaughtered, their pelts removed and the carcasses fed to swine. They could have been cured by a

few dippings in a medicated bath but, by this
time, sheep had fallen to one dollar per head so
that the cost of cure would have been a large per
cent of the selling price. The footrot, the scab
and an atrophied market utterly destroyed the
sheep industry in the state of Iowa and where
thousands of sheep once grazed scarcely one can
now be found. On the other hand, at the close of
1864 fat hogs sold for as high as twelve and one-
half cents per pound live weight; and it was said
that one man sold a single fat porker for a little
over one hundred dollars. I have gone into such
details that you may understand the downs and ups
of farming in those times and also to show how I
was getting some more education in practical
agriculture.

Nor is farming less uncertain at the present
time. At this writing in January, 1910, un-
bleached Sultana raisins are nominally quoted at
two and one-half cents per pound — the fact is, no
bids can be obtained for them at any price. Two
years ago this same class of raisins sold readily, delivered at the station, at seven to nine cents per
pound. So does he who farms go merrily both up
hill and down; so fluctuates the farmer's business;
but he always quotes the big returns, not having

become wise enough yet to figure in the lean years with the fat ones.

Having briefly outlined how we lived, what we ate, what we produced and the prices we received for staple farm crops, I may return to more intimate matters. Spurred on by adversity and prosperity, at last I began to think seriously and to a purpose. I was no longer looking over my shoulder to see if the county house was in sight but, western-fashion, was trying to purchase an adjoining farm. I was now bent upon the production of livestock on a large scale. I thought to pack most of the farm products inside the skins of well-bred animals for more could be realized in that way at that time than by selling crude products. When the scheme to buy land came to naught, I planned to build a barn. I had so far made shift with enclosed sheds made of poles, slabs, brush and straw, which served well enough in dry weather but were far from sufficient in rainy weather. The new barn had a stone basement surmounted by twenty foot posts and was a veritable wonder for the time and locality.

I remember distinctly digging a ditch one day in hard ground, after I had begun to think just a little. Sitting on its rim mopping the perspiration from my face while resting my aching back, thoughts something like these came to me: " Roberts, you are in the right place for you have not yet skill nor money to enter into a wider life; but someday you will climb out of this ditch and stay out, and leave digging for some other young fellow to learn what a day's manual labor really means. He who would intelligently direct must first have learned how to serve."

I had begun to feel that somehow I must get clear of this exacting muscular labor, but eighty acres of arable land could not be made to support a mere planner and pay laborers at the same time to do the heavy work. The farm was like the turkey of the man from Missouri — too large for one and not quite enough for two. Animal industry, I knew by experience, was profitable and it was beginning to dawn on my awakening mind, that through livestock, the productivity of the land could be maintained, even increased, and a good profit secured. In this I saw a surcease from too exacting toil and a possibility of making myself worthy to be the representative of my neighbors in some honorable position at the State Capitol. I wonder how many other ambitious young men have caught that political bee in their bonnets, who never arrived at the Capitol! Although most of these dreams came to nothing they helped to rest my back, to broaden my vision and to improve my judgment.

The growth of my religious life deserves to be recorded. During my first year's residence in Iowa I became greatly interested in the study of the Bible. Instead of going to church I spent my Sundays in an honest endeavor to comprehend some of the vital truths which that Book of Books contains. I soon discovered that many things therein were " too great for me." But I did not allow these to becloud the perfect and simple rules of life I found there, although they were sometimes clothed in Oriental imagery. After I had studied for about a year I concluded that my studies could be greatly advanced by joining some organization; and looking into the matter carefully, I concluded that I could work with the Baptists most cordially and so became a member of that church.

The Bible study not only interested me but profoundly stimulated my intellectual life. When we moved to the farm six miles away from Mount Pleasant, it was inconvenient to attend church or other assemblages often, but the Highland schoolhouse was only a mile and a half away and so with a few neighbors, a farmers club was organized which, I am told, is still an active society. In the spring of our first year on the farm a Sunday school was started in the same schoolhouse — for the benefit of the children it was proclaimed, but I am persuaded that the grown-ups received more benefit than the children. Having been elected superintendent, I was stimulated to keep myself well-versed in the lessons. When fall came the question of adjournment for the winter was raised, and it occurred to me why not continue through the winter, meeting at night as the club did. The suggestion found favor and as long as I resided in that locality, the all-year-round Sunday school prospered.

As to adult membership, the club and the Sunday school were mostly composed of the same persons and, being successful in two undertakings, we attempted a third. The County Agricultural Fair Association had died of anemia some time before. We set about resuscitating it for we believed the country was now sufficiently settled up to maintain it. Here was my first effort to make a public address. Although the printed copy of it is now lost, the main ideas still linger in my memory. One of them was: " Build the smokestacks and the grain-stacks in sight of each other! " The idea grew out of the fact that in those days we sent nearly everything we produced to distant markets and a large proportion of our necessary supplies came from the far east or from Europe. Another idea of that paper was: "Improve the highways by underground drains laid with hard-burned, round drain tiles." The summer had been unusually wet that year and it was hard for us to get to town and harder for us to stay at home. Our reapers would sometimes mire down in the grain fields; and often had to be left there half-buried for want of fulcrums on which to place levers. Thus much of the harvest had to be cut with grain cradles — a very laborious proceeding.

The following year we made a visit to my old home in New York and I brought back with me two drain tiles, hoping to get some brick-maker interested in manufacturing them. It is probable that these were the first drain tiles carried beyond the Mississippi river. Since then, in many places both in Iowa and Illinois, the public highways have been underdrained with tile to carry off the rain, for water is a greater destroyer of dirt roads than all other enemies combined.

A man may set out on a definite track but he seldom anticipates the switch which may shunt him off onto another — thus it has been with me. I never got started on a fairly straight track but that I was sure to be shunted onto another, and one which was apt to be poorly ballasted. In the latter part of May, 1869, as I was giving the last touch to my fine new barn by building a cupola on it just for looks, I heard a voice at the top of the ladder, and turning, I saw the red head of O. H. P. Buchanan just above the eaves. Said he: "Come down from there, young man, I have better work for you to do."

It seemed that Mr. Buchanan had shortly before been appointed a Trustee of the Iowa State College of Agriculture and Mechanic Arts, usually known as the "I. A. C.," which was situated at Ames, Story County, Iowa. The Superintendent of the College Farm and the Secretary of the Board of Trustees was a high-tempered Scotchman who had a habit of resigning on the slightest pretext. The patience of the Trustees had at last given out and they were looking for someone to take Superintendent Thompson's place. Mr. Buchanan wished to recommend me for the position; but at first I declined to be switched off onto this new, unknown track for I still had the livestock tick in my bonnet. Though I finally consented to allow him to present my name, I declined to furnish him with any commendatory letters.

When the matter came up before the Board there were many applicants and I have been told that I was elected in the following manner: One of the Trustees, a physician, noted among other things for his strong language, remarked: " That pile of recommendations isn't worth a damn — I can get twice as many certifying that I am a good Methodist minister. Buchanan, do you know this man Roberts and what stuff he is made of?" Receiving a satisfactory answer from Mr. Buchanan, the Board unanimously elected me to the position.

To my great surprise I was asked to take charge at once, and that of necessity left Mrs. Roberts — with the help of a hired lad and a neighbor — to get in the harvest on the home farm. And so, as it turned out, I never pitched a load of hay with my fine new horse-fork nor did an hour's work in the New Barn, which was great enough in my estimation to be spelled with capitals.

Leaving home at once, I arrived at the College in June, gathered the harvest there and then, returning to my own farm, threshed and marketed the grain, stored the household goods in the upper rooms and found a tenant. With homesick hearts and with every expectation of returning in a year or two, we with our two children left the home where we had suffered much hardship and done much heavy labor but where we had also planned and saved and been happy — where our first son, Perry Buchanan Roberts, was born and where I had received the foundation of my agricultural education. Little as we imagined it then we were never to return to live in that humble house which we had loved so much.

We arrived at the College in August, 1869, and took possession of a large, two-story brick farmhouse. We were expected to board and often to lodge from six to eight workmen, the Trustees when the Board was in session, the Professors who were not yet provided with dwellings, and the indoor employes — a mixed company sometimes amounting to thirty persons. As Secretary of the Board of Trustees, I was an employe of the State — the Commonwealth's watch dog; as Superintendent I managed the farm. The salary of the former was one thousand, of the latter seven hundred and fifty dollars per year with board, rooms, heat, light and washing for myself and family included. Mrs. Roberts superintended the farm household, her salary being included in the above. On the whole the salaries were liberal considering the newness of the College and the country.

I remember that the kitchen door, which faced on what was then the main drive, opened on the very line of the road. The wood for the stoves had been deposited in saw-log lengths at the kitchen door to be chopped up into stove-lengths. There, cutting stove-wood, I first saw Mr. W. T. Hornaday, who is now the Curator of the Bronx Park Museum and Director of the New York Zoological Gardens. I little thought then that that stubby, bronzed lad at the wood-pile would ever attain so useful and distinguished a position as he now occupies.

All college students were then required to work two and one-half hours daily, being paid an average wage of about eight cents an hour. From forty to fifty were detailed each morning to the farm. Having more hands than I could easily find work for, I decided to clear up the campus, which consisted of about ninety acres. The heterogeneous rubbish due to many changes and much building was gathered in wagon loads, sorted and piled up. The knotty logs at the kitchen door were moved from their ancient resting-place and added to the useless scrap pile; and the vast accumulation of chip manure was hauled away, which widened the drive-way from about twelve to its original forty feet. When the scrap pile was burning one evening, the President came rushing over, fearing that a building was on fire, but seeing what it was, he remarked: "Mr. Superintendent are you not burning up some things of value?" I was, probably, but I was determined to fix that old rubbish so that it could not be used again to clutter up the campus.

That part of the farm which lay between the buildings and the village of Ames, about two miles away, was low land and subject to overflow in the spring for short periods, from a crooked, sluggish stream. Weeds, from four to eight feet tall, covered the face of this wild, hummocky pasture, which was only sparsely set with coarse grasses. In this pasture several fine full-blooded animals which had been purchased at long figures in Illinois, New York and Canada, were kept with other cattle; but no one could have told whether the cattle were scrubs or Duchesses and Dukes, because of the weeds. As this land abutted the causeway across the lowland over which the main road approached the college, it was a great eyesore and gave a bad impression of our farming methods; so I sent a sturdy Norwegian, with a team of mules hitched to an old mower, to mow it.

Sometimes Lars rode and sometimes he didn't but when that field was mowed I paid my respects to him and the mules. Warm rains in September caused the grass, which had not seen clear daylight for years, to spring up and grow lusciously; and when the Board of Trustees travelled over it in coming from the station to the College, they could not help observing with approval the change from an unkept, weedy lowland, to a green pasture dotted with fine Shorthorn, Devon and Ayrshire cattle.

I might as well finish the history of that low-land field just here, although it will take me into the second and third years of my stay at the I. A. C. The next spring it was plowed for the first time. The accepted method of subduing wild prairie land was then to use a "breaker"; but the plow we used was not a breaker and hence would not kink the furrows so that the wild grass would "burn out," that is, perish for want of moisture during the summer. Our plow laid the furrows flat and unless something more was done the last state of that field might be worse than the first. The students, with axes in hand, followed down every fourth furrow-slice and at intervals of about four feet cut a slit in the sod, dropped some grains of corn and then cut another slit by the side of the first one which served to close the first one and to cover the corn. Before and after the seed was planted the ground was harrowed and re-harrowed again and again but with little apparent effect — the sod was too tenacious. But I have yet to see more roughage — along with a few ears — grown per acre than grew on that marshy field, and it was just what was needed for our many cattle after the prairie grasses had dried up in the fall.

Mrs. Ellen Tupper, the College lecturer on Bee Culture, highly recommended Alsike or Swedish clover, not only as a superb honey plant but as a good forage plant, for low land. The flowers of Alsike, like those of white clover, are so shallow that honey bees can secure their sweets, while red clover flowers are so deep that only bumblebees can reach the honey they contain. This tough ground was therefore re-plowed the following spring and two bushels of imported Alsike clover seed — no seed could then be obtained in the United States — at a cost of thirty dollars per bushel was sowed. I have no words to describe the beauty and the perfume of that field of clover; I have never since raised so good a crop of clover of any kind. But I take little credit for it, for it was just one of those fortunate little things which come to us sometimes from following a friendly suggestion.

My purpose in relating these details is not so much to adorn my tale as to point a moral: little duties well performed often lead to larger things. For, when the Board of Trustees convened in the late fall of 1869, the first resolution they passed made me Professor of Agriculture. That widened road where the log pile had been, that burned rubbish from the campus and that beautiful green lowland pasture had won their confidence. I was certainly most fortunate; here was the livestock farm which I had longed for so many years and a great farm it was, although much of it was still in virgin prairie. There was on the place about a hundred head of cattle; two small flocks of sheep, one long-wooled and one selected fine-wooled; the possibilities of rearing a hundred Berkshire pigs yearly; and six hundred acres of prairie and woodland, to which was added later two hundred acres more. It will be seen that the I. A. C. started out on purely agricultural lines and it is because it has adhered rather closely to them that it has risen to first rank among those of its kind.

While enjoying the practical work of the farm I found here another opportunity for self-education,

The lecturer on agriculture, Dr. Townsend, had gone to the State University of Ohio where he did valuable work. He was a man of unusual ability and his scope of knowledge was wide and in some lines profound. As there were few trained men in agriculture at that time, his position was not easy to fill. One day President Welch asked me why I could not teach agriculture; I replied because I did not know how. "But," said he, "Can't you tell the boys how you have been doing things — I understand you have long been a successful school teacher." The President carried out his suggestion, as he usually did, and I began to tell the students what I knew about farming. It did not take me long to run short of material and then I began to consult the library. I might as well have looked for cranberries on the Rocky Mountains as for material for teaching agriculture in that library.

Thus, fortunately, I was driven to take the class to the field and farm, there to study plants, animals and tillage at first hand. So again I was shunted onto the right track by sheer necessity and ever since I have kept the rails hot on that particular spur. Much of the illustrative material necessary for agricultural teaching cannot be assembled in the class room and so I fell into the habit of taking

the students to view good and poor farms; to see
fine herds and scrub herds in the country round-
about, even though they sometimes had to travel
on freight cars. I suppose I was the first teacher
of agriculture to make use, in a large way, of the
fields and the stables of the countryside as laboratories. I simply found myself in the position of
the boy and the woodchuck when a visit from the
minister was expected — it was a ground-hog case.

One day, being short of lecture material, I went
to the fields and gathered a great armful of the
common weed pests. Handing them round to the
class I asked for the common and the botanical
names, and the methods of eradication—I received
only two answers and those quite inadequate —
although these twenty-five young men had spent
most of their waking hours since childhood in
fields where there were more weeds than useful
plants. This experiment provided material for a
week's classroom talk and led me to place still more
emphasis on field laboratory work — " walks and
talks "— we called them. When the subject of the
horse — breeding, age, care and management —
came up, I went again to the library for help. But
the horse books were all out of date, chiefly filled
with information about hunters, jumpers, and

6

racers and their wonderful feats, and a little about the European draft breeds which were then in process of formation. Although I found in them much "horsey" talk and brag, I found almost nothing that would be of use to an American farmer.

Here was a great opening for original work. It appeared to me that farmers should know how to tell the age of a horse with a reasonable degree of certainty; and hearing that many rather young horses had recently died of an epidemic in the immediate neighborhood, I had two farm hands dig them up and preserved the heads and some special parts and such limbs as had been malformed by disease. By careful inquiry I was able to fix accurately the ages of most of these animals. Arranging my material on a workbench in the open, I placed the class on the windward side and taught them the fundamental principles of horse dentition. I have found it difficult to give students a WORKING knowledge of this subject and so have given great attention to it in my book on The Horse.

These few illustrations will serve to show how difficult it was in those early days to teach agriculture and to find proper illustrative material. There was no well-worn trail to follow as there is now, and though the work might have been criticised, happily for me there was no one then fitted for the task. Of the subject of teaching in general I will speak later; of my own teaching, looking at it from this distance, it may fairly be said that it was practical and thorough as far as it went, but stopped far short of what is given in similar courses today. It served, however, to blaze the way for those who followed.

About forty rods from the farm house stood " The College," as it was then designated. It was a large brick building with two long wings and the only college building when I first arrived. In the basement of one wing was a large dining hall and the kitchen; on the first floor the chapel and the administrative offices; while the third and fourth floor were occupied by students. In the other wing was housed the library and the museum, and the upper two stories, as in the other wing, were given up to students. The women students, who were admitted from the beginning, roomed in one end of the main building on the lower floors. There were between three and four hundred students.

This was a diverse crowd to feed, govern and keep at work. After trying a few experiments the general government of the students was put in the hands of a judiciary committee composed of the President and four members of the faculty. All major infractions of rules were tried before this body; and their findings were read before the full faculty at stated periods; but all minor affairs — infractions of the ordinary rules of conduct in the classroom and in and about the campus, were tried before a student council composed of upper class men and class women. The person to be tried had the right to select one of his fellow pupils to assist him in defense, while one of the council acted in the capacity of attorney for the College. Only once during my knowledge of it, did the decisions of the student council fail to be approved by the faculty.

After seeing many experiments in student government; and after sitting in a faculty of more than fifty members for hours to try a single student for some petty infraction which often involved no turpitude but only thoughtlessness, I am convinced that this method was the most just, expedient and satisfactory of any I am acquainted with. General Geddes who was military commandant and steward, and in charge of order within the building, was an able, kind but very exacting officer. The success of his administration was due in part to wide experience and in part to its military character, with the uniforms and the red tape left out.

Professor C. E. Bessey (now of the University of Nebraska) was often "officer of the day," or rather during study hours from 8 to 10 o'clock in the evening, and made the night and morning inspections. The rising bell rang at 5.30 a. m.; breakfast was at 6 and inspection at 6.45 when students' rooms had to be in order or there was prompt reckoning. All unexcused students reported for work at 7 a. m. The officers of the day as well as others were obliged to make a daily written report to the President. The students were required and the faculty requested to meet at 4.30 p. m. in the Chapel where a short reading from the scriptures and prayer was followed by directions for the next day's work and by various notices. From 5 to 8 o'clock was given to supper and recreation. On Saturdays no duties except special details were required; on Sunday attendance at the morning service was treated the same as a class exercise. Strange as it may now seem, all of these religious exercises were attended with apparent pleasure, perhaps because the students were allowed to remain afterward for a quiet social hour.

The boys and girls were not allowed to mingle freely except during recreation hours and after Sunday chapel; and no scandal and few breaches of social discipline occurred during the four years of my stay.

President A. S. Welch was a keen, cultivated gentleman, of very pleasant manners, patient under defeat and usually able to turn defeat into victory. That he successfully built an excellent college out on the lonely, wind-swept prairies by the track of an uncompleted railway, marks him as a great organizer. That he was able to govern and mould that mass of crude boys and girls and inexperienced professors — picked up at first almost at random, as they had to be — into an efficient educational institution, proves him a man of rare executive ability. Had his lot been cast in a larger field and in a later time, President Welch would have been accounted by posterity one of the great college presidents of America.

President Welch organized and conducted the first Farmers' Institutes in the United States. Associated with him was Mrs. Ellen Tupper — "The Bee Woman" — Professors Jones, Mathews, Bessey and Roberts, and our experiences were those of pioneers. On one occasion after an evening meeting at Council Bluffs, Iowa, the President

and I were invited to go home with a farmer who
lived five miles distant. About midnight we retired to a room on the walls of which you might
have written your name in the glittering frost. I
slept with the President and when we touched the
icy sheets, he remarked: " Roberts, I guess we
will have to spoon " — and we spooned.

I have often wondered since then why this large
family of faculty and students, housed mostly in
one building, got on so well together. Was it
because the nearest town was small and had no
saloons? Or because the boys had not yet conceived the idea that colleges are chiefly to promote
athletics and nocturnal episodes? Or because the
system was exceptionally good; or because of the
exceptional ability of its chief executive officers —
or perhaps because of all these combined? One
thing is certain: the President did not go fishing in
term-time nor up and down the country hunting
honors and notoriety. With few exceptions the
faculty was composed of young, able, progressive,
industrious teachers; and with a president at the
head who always knew what was going on, and
who not only had the courage to point out defects
but the wisdom to see and appreciate good work
and the sense to praise it; the instruction was of a

high grade. It was, perhaps, the best that could be obtained at that time and under the conditions which then prevailed.

The requirements for admission were necessarily low and much preparatory instruction had to be given; but when once prepared, I have yet to find pupils who made such rapid advancement as did those eager, unspoiled students from the prairie farms. Later on many of the students who came to us were fitted for entrance by our own upper classmen and were therefore superior to those who had been confused by a multitude of subjects badly taught.

The college year began the last of February and closed the end of the following October with only a few days vacation in July. There were two reasons for placing the long vacation in the winter; first, the method of warming the College building by the Routan system was an expensive failure; and second, the winter vacation gave an opportunity for all qualified students to teach in the public schools where they were much in demand. This arrangement proved advantageous in many ways. The secondary schools were benefited; attention was drawn to the College; prospective pupils received a better preparation along the

lines required for entrance to college; and the
student teachers acquired experience and secured
funds to pay their expenses.

I wish that the methods of instruction, practice
and government which prevailed in my time at the
I. A. C. could be written down in detail and sent
out for the use of the farm schools which are now
springing up; which of necessity will be conducted
under similar conditions and will receive pupils
not unlike those that attended the Iowa College
in the beginning.   They should be fundamentally
correct when applied to institutions of a similar
character.

In the third year of my stay at Ames, internal
troubles began — discord between the Trustees
and some members of the faculty.   William A.
Anthony, the Professor of Physics, had made ar-
rangements to go east and study during the winter
vacation; but the Trustees required him to remain
at the College to attend to the plumbing of some
of the new buildings under construction.   This
meant his doing a large part of the work with his
own hands for skilled workmen could seldom be
had in this locality.   He obeyed at this time but
it was the straw which caused this man of exceptionally diversified and eminent qualifications to

accept another position soon afterward at Cornell University.

Shortly after this there arose other troubles of a more serious nature. The State had made a liberal appropriation for a Chemical building and about the time the foundations for it were in place, it was discovered that the College Treasurer, who was also State Treasurer, had defaulted for a large sum — and the building was stopped. He was not under bonds — this formality having been overlooked — and recriminations arose in the effort to fix and shift the responsibility for the mistake. Several members of the faculty arrayed themselves against the President, charging him with dereliction in certain matters and with performing unauthorized acts in the general management of the College. In other words, a few professors tried to unseat the President but were themselves unseated finally at a special meeting of the Board of Trustees. Most of the members of the State Assembly, and virtually every newspaper in the State, took an active interest on one side or the other of this controversy. I have seldom witnessed so bitter a fight and it was very difficult for me to keep out of it.

In 1873 my eyes began to fail from over-work

and especially from over-study at night; and, having a horror of being mixed up in a factional fight and Mrs. Roberts' duties at the farm house having become too burdensome, I handed in my resignation. Professor Anthony was by this time at Cornell University. He had kept himself well informed as to the trouble at the I. A. C. and knew long before I resigned that I was far from being satisfied with the outlook for the future.

As I remember, it was in October, 1873, that I received a letter from him asking if I would consider favorably a call to Cornell University. I replied that I was tired out with over-work and wrangling, and was only waiting for a suitable time to go back to my farm. In answer to this he wrote asking me to formulate a plan for the organization of the College of Agriculture at Cornell which he might show to President Andrew D. White. I forwarded a somewhat lengthy statement and about two weeks after this, Vice-President Russell of Cornell came to the College at Ames prepared to discuss these plans and to offer me a position as Superintendent of the University farm and Assistant Professor of Agriculture.

At that time the Cornell year was divided into three terms, running from September to June. I declined to consider a plan by which I should have no vacation, unless the salary was increased. I also declined to take my vacation in mid-summer, since I was certain that the farm could not be successfully carried on if I should spend the three busiest months away from the University. It was agreed finally — in case I should be appointed — that I might take a vacation of three months in winter and lecture only in the fall and spring terms.

When the fall meeting of the Board of Trustees was held at the I. A. C., in November, 1873, I had not yet heard anything from Cornell and as my resignation was in President Welch's hands, and his also in the Trustees' hands, I was planning to return to my farm at Mount Pleasant. At the first session of the Board a resolution was passed vacating all positions in the college. Re-convening after dinner in a more reasonable frame of mind, the Board proceeded to the election of a President, a faculty and other officers. President Welch and all of his co-workers except three full professors, were re-elected to the positions which they had previously filled. Thus I was on in the morning, off at noon, and on again by evening.

I again offered my resignation to take effect in January, 1874, and it was accepted. A few days later while the Board of Trustees was still in session, I received a telegram informing me of my appointment to the position of Assistant Professor of Agriculture at Cornell University with a full professor's salary and the promise that no full professor should be placed over me. I showed the message to my old friend, Trustee Buchanan, and with it in his hand he preceded me to the supper table and introduced me to the Board and the company as the Professor of Agriculture at Cornell University. I believe that was one of the happiest moments of his life. It was he who had secured my appointment at the I. A. C. when I was not competent to fill it — that is, he had taken me on trust — and he had stood by me and seen me grow. Now came the fulfilled joy of having his judgment of this " diamond in the rough " justified.

The appointment pleased me, as it might any ambitious young man, for it was a testimonial to my growth and ability, and yet I hesitated to accept it. I was in a discouraged frame of mind partly from over-work and partly from a lack of appreciation on the part of those whom my work had been designed to benefit as well as by an increasing sense of the difficulties that would have to be met at Cornell. I had begun to lose faith in the college method of raising the business of farming to an intelligent and dignified calling. But fortunately, my friend Mr. Buchanan had a wider view and a stronger faith than I in the new agricultural education, and when I asked his advice about accepting the position he said: "If you don't accept it I'll never forgive you — it's the great opportunity of your life — don't hesitate a moment even though your title will be only that of Assistant Professor. If you can't change that for a full professorship very soon then you are not the man I think you are." And that's the way I came to go to Cornell — as I supposed perhaps for only a year or two, for even yet I dreamed of going back to my own farm and being independent.

Again the switch had been turned and again I had been shunted on to another road. At Ames I had enjoyed the farm end of my work greatly, but I had not become much interested in purely educational lines; that development was to come later. My own judgment and inclination said, go back to Mount Pleasant; but my trusted friend said, go to Cornell — it is an opportunity which comes to a man but once in a lifetime — you can get a big livestock farm anytime. And so I set out not knowing whither I was going.

PROFESSOR ROBERTS AT SEVENTY

After thirty years as Dean and Director at Cornell

SECTION III

LIFE AND WORK AT CORNELL UNIVERSITY

———

(1874—1903

LIFE AND WORK AT CORNELL UNIVERSITY

On January 1, 1874, we left Ames, and after attending to some private business en route, reached Ithaca, New York, on February first. There we secured rooms in *Cascadilla*, a dreary stone building which had been erected for a Sanatorium and was then used for an apartment house; and set up housekeeping for the fifth time and only thirty miles from the old homestead on Cayuga Lake which I had left nearly twenty years earlier. I and my family were plain people off the western prairies; and perhaps because of it and more, perhaps, because agriculture was then regarded by most of the classically educated members of the Cornell faculty as quite unworthy of a place in education beside the traditional subjects of the curriculum, we suffered a sort of social neglect and felt ourselves in an alien atmosphere. The contempt for such practical subjects and their teachers was shared to some extent for a number of years by many of the professors of technical departments who were not highly cultivated outside their own fields.

The University farm was under a lease which did not expire until the following April and there was very little teaching to be done, there being only three senior students in agriculture, and they having already taken their technical training under my predecessor, Professor McCandless. There were two, John L. Stone and William R. Lazenby — both of whom are now well-known professors in Agriculture, the one at Cornell and the other at Ohio University — and a few strays to whom I gave an hour of instruction per day, five days in the week for the rest of that year. This left me plenty of time to look over the situation and to realize how different our conditions were to be from those in Iowa.

From an ample farmhouse to three living rooms in Cascadilla Place; from an 800-acre farm, where in one year I had raised 5,000 bushels of corn, to one of less than 100 acres of arable land; from a herd of 100 cattle, representing four breeds, to one of twelve miserable cows; from setting fifty to seventy-five students at work every morning to directing five hired men; from large classes of enthusiastic pupils and ample classrooms to a museum for a lecture room and a pocket edition of a class — such were the comparisons that I instinctively made in those first months.

The history of the University farm and the attempts at agricultural education were even more
disheartening. I learned that the farm had first
been placed in the hands of a Mr. Spaulding, a
man of delicate health who of necessity spent most
of his time in summer at some health resort; the
inevitable result was neglect, followed by weak
apologies for its unsightly conditions. In the hope
of bettering matters, the farm was then leased to
a Cortland farmer who moved into Cascadilla —
in those days everybody moved into "The
Bastile" as the students dubbed it — and he was
supposed to give the University one-third of the
proceeds of the land.

Meanwhile, President Andrew D. White, while
in Europe, had selected Professor James Law, a
young Scotchman, to be the head of the Veterinary
Department — a department that has now grown
into the State Veterinary College and is one of the
best of its kind in America. About 1872 the
President also called an Irishman, a Mr. McCandless from Glasnevin to the Chair of Agriculture.
Professor McCandless declined to have anything
to do with the farm until a large barn had been
built after his own plans. Ezra Cornell was determined to get the Department of Agriculture

properly started and himself furnished the money to build it. But both the barn and the foreign professor were failures.

The barn was a large, expensive structure, two stories and basement, located on a slight incline. The second story or top of the barn was to be entered by a long, steep earth causeway, which would require at least a thousand yards of earth in its construction. The plan was to use one-horse Irish carts which could easily be turned round inside the barn when the carts were unloaded. I never built this causeway, but I completed the barn after altering it in some important particulars, and it never ceased to be a monstrosity. It burned down about 1890 — peace be to its ashes!

Mr. McCandless had purchased in Ireland several hundred dollars worth of farm implements, which I am quite unable to describe, so queer and clumsy were they, and which were quite useless in the United States. The greater part of them were burned up in the barn and those that escaped were placed among the other antiquities.

Of Professor McCandless it may be said, however, that he excelled all of his successors in good looks. He was a really noble looking man, soft-handed and always perfectly groomed. He only stayed at Cornell one year and afterward went to Guelph, Ontario, Canada, to be the head of the Provincial Agricultural School. About two years later a Government Committee investigated this institution and he was dismissed.

It was upon the heels of these mistakes and after five years of such mismanagement that I took charge of the Cornell farm and the courses in Agriculture. Although I had been led to believe that there was an appropriation of $10,000 for putting the College on its feet, I found that this had disappeared and that everything was in a most discouraging condition. Coming as I did from the Iowa College where I had been doing things in a large way — if not always in the best way — to New York which I had looked upon as a great State, and to a University founded upon broad and ideal lines, my expectations had been high; and when I discovered the true condition of affairs, they sank low — lower, perhaps than even these untoward conditions warranted. It did not take me long to decide that one year at Cornell would be enough unless many things which I could scarcely hope for, should come to pass.

Since to look gloomy and to complain would not help matters, I set to work to eradicate disease and filth from the dairy, to repair buildings and fences, and to clean up things generally. And quite to my surprise, things began to happen which made the situation more tolerable. In the Register of 1873–4 Professor Caldwell's name had been printed as "Instructor" and mine as "Assistant Professor;" but in 1874–5 Professor Caldwell was made full Professor of Agricultural Chemistry and I Professor of Agriculture. This promotion showed that my efforts during that first year were being appreciated.

I think it was in the fall of that first year that President A. S. Welch of the Iowa State College of Agriculture and Mechanic Arts, came to make me a visit. Before leaving he said to me that while I was at the Iowa College a degree mattered little to me for there I was judged, as other men were in the West, by their works; but that in the East, a title would be a help to me. He offered to bring this matter to the attention of the Iowa Faculty on the ground that I had had years of study and experience, although I had not followed the regular courses, and he was kind enough to say that I had earned a degree. He thought it possible that they would give me an honorary one.

Shortly afterward, by a unanimous vote, the Faculty of the Iowa College recommended to the

Board of Trustees that I be given the degree of Master of Agriculture, and the Board adopted the recommendation. This was the first degree of M.Agr. ever given by them or, in fact, given by any college in the United States.

The President of Cornell University, Andrew D. White, took the greatest interest in my work from the beginning; and as I became better acquainted with Cornell and with his plans I think I must have acquired the " Cornell spirit," for by the end of the first year I was loath to give up my place. So much had been done to encourage me and to give my department as good standing as it could have, considering the circumstances, that I reconsidered my determination to return to my farm in Iowa. I realized that the time had come for me to make a well-digested plan for my future life and for my children and to pursue it steadfastly to the end. I saw that there was a larger future here both for them and for me than there would be if I should become the livestock farmer in Iowa that I had planned to be. By this time maturity and a broader outlook had caused me to understand the possibilities of agricultural education and I determined to lay the foundations of a College of Agriculture such as had never been conceived.

On the 1st of April, 1874, I took an inventory of all the property belonging to the farm, a copy of which I filed with the University Treasurer — the first ever taken by any department of the University. The next year orders went out to every department to file such lists of property with values affixed. I also introduced a system of farm accounts so that not only the loss and gain of the whole undertaking but of each subdivision of it might be ascertained — an idea which I had brought from the Iowa College. This farm accounting was so carefully worked out even then that it is still followed with scarcely a change except in minor details.

It revealed many things unseen before. It appeared that the dairy might be made to more than pay expenses; and the work stock also, for they found employment in other departments when not needed on the farm; and this, in spite of the fact that all the animals were in wretched condition. There were ten milch cows that had among them only twenty-two milkable teats and the Veterinarian did not have to be called in to know that the herd was infected with tuberculosis. One of the work oxen was sound and strong but it took most of his strength to hold up his mate. There was a stallion of noted Arabian lineage which had been donated to the University and was said to be worth $15,000 but I have always thought that the decimal point ought to have been placed two figures to the left.   He had not been out of his box stall for two years.   Although he was the sire of a few colts he was withdrawn from service perhaps because his colts did not have legs enough on which to place the curbs, ring-bones, spavins, and deformities, which he was capable of transmitting. When we took that Arab of the Desert out of his stall and rode him, he fell dead!

The renter of the University Farm owned a farm in Cortland on which he kept a herd of short-horns and a flock of Merino sheep; but his public boarding house table at Cascadilla Place was provided with milk and meats from the pick-ups and semi-uddered cows brought from his own farm to the University.   And that's the kind of food we fed upon at " The Bastile " in those early days!

I am giving this circumstantial account of the unhappy conditions which I found on taking charge of the University Farm that you may better understand how difficult the problems were which I had, by implication at least, promised to solve.   So far from being a model to the farmers of the State the farm was under the shadow of dishonesty and mismanagement, and I was a stranger in the land of my birth. Vice-President Russell once remarked to me that there was nothing he dreaded so much as to have a farmer drop in and ask to be shown over the " Model Farm." Many a time I looked back longingly to my Iowa farm and while load after load of stone was being taken from the fields at Cornell, I remembered the black soil of the prairies; but having set my hand to this task, I would not draw back.

One of the first things I did was to have the immense accumulation of farmyard manure hauled out and spread thickly on the corn ground that was to be. The manure was strawey, the spring wet and late, the ground undrained and clayey; and after waiting for it to dry it was plowed at last a little too moist and quite as deep as I was used to plowing the friable, warm soil of the prairies. It will be seen that I made three serious mistakes at once in one cornfield on that farm that was to be a "model;" but apparently no one observed them but myself and the corn. Afterwards when I had drained this field and otherwise improved its productive power, we were able to raise in one propitious year, over eighty bushels of shelled corn per acre, although the soil was too clayey and the climate too cool for the most successful corn culture.

That first year a field of oats was sown with seed which was already in the granary. The grain ripened early, but did not yield half as much as I thought it should in a climate so well adapted to oat culture as that of western New York. So after harvest, I made a visit to some farms near Ovid, a town about twenty miles down the lake and not far from my boyhood home. Here the oat harvest was just beginning and the crop was abundant. This was in part attributable to the beech and maple land which was naturally much better adapted for oats than the pine and hemlock lands about Ithaca. The next spring I secured seed from Ovid of these " Dog-tail " oats and the following year the yield per acre on the University Farm was much larger.

I became acquainted with Jacob Bates, a neighboring farmer, who not only had good land but was expert in cultivating it. He was sowing two bushels of oats and one-half bushel of barley mixed, per acre, and made the claim that he had raised one hundred bushels per acre of this mixture. I adopted his practice with most successful results. The barley shoots up ahead of the oats and becomes well developed in grains before the oats throws up its seed stalks and heads out. Then when it does, the barley is hidden and supported till harvest time. I tried year after year to excel this neighbor but only once succeeded in raising a trifle more than eighty bushels per acre. However, I did succeed while at Cornell, in more than doubling the average yield secured by my predecessors.

Not long after I came to Cornell I made a visit to Fayette, Seneca County, and while there I drew out of those superior Dutch farmers about all they knew of New York agriculture. It must be remembered that almost all of my adult life had been spent on the prairies of the West and all I knew of eastern farming had been learned in my boyhood at East Varick. So once again I had to become a painstaking student in order to fit myself to cope with New York conditions.

Let me go back to the history of that oat field! After the first oat harvest the land was prepared and seeded in September to winter wheat. About two weeks afterwards six quarts of timothy seed per acre were sowed among the young wheat plants. Parenthetically I may say, that if grass seed is sown at the time of seeding to wheat and the wheat should be injured by the winter, the timothy, being hardier and more vigorous, will have the advantage and the harvest is likely to show as much headed-out timothy as wheat. In the spring six quarts to the acre of mixed red and alsike clover seed were also sowed.

To harvest the wheat, I purchased a self twine-binder, which I think was the first in that region. We had a regular two-ring circus cutting that wheat. When the machine ran parallel to the hills it would upset if someone did not hold down the grain-wheel; then we started straight up from the bottom of the hill with my carriage team hitched on ahead of the three-horse team; but now the grain would slide off the endless apron unless someone held it on with a hand rake. In spite of every care the grain went to the binder much tangled; then the binder kicked — or rather refused to kick — the sheaves out of the goose-neck.

Mr. W. R. Lazenby, who was then a senior in College and is now a Professor in Ohio University, helped to draw in the grain one torrid August day. The first load upset and the wagon with it and it was a couple of hours before a part of a load arrived at the barn. Mr. Lazenby took a drink of water, mopped his face, and made this wise remark, which had been evolved out of his difficulties: "Professor, I don't believe it is profitable to raise wheat on that field." And I promised him then and there that it should never be plowed again even if I stayed there a quarter of a century.

And I kept my word although I stayed there nearly thirty years. The next year the field was mowed and ever after it was pastured. This is the field known as the "Roberts' Pasture" which now for more than a quarter of a century, has attracted much attention, though I never did anything wonderful to it — I merely treated it liberally, for I believe that pastures and boys, alike, should be treated not too niggardly. Only to-day I met a wealthy man's fourteen-year-old son going to see Mr. Paulan's free display of aviation, thirty miles away. He had been given only just money enough to pay steam-car fare, so I paid his street-car fare rather than see him walk a mile to the station. That boy may fly from home later on as his elder brother did, merely because he was not generously treated.

The back field of the farm when I came to Cornell, was in timothy which had been mowed for several years previously, but ox-eyed daisies had virtually taken possession of it. Discussing this apparent failure with a neighboring farmer, he remarked casually that he would be willing to gather the crop for half the hay — " daisies made pretty fair hay!" He was right and I gained a new idea. That field later, after it was drained and coaxed, produced a little over forty-five bushels of wheat per acre — the best crop I ever raised.*

About 1890, much discussion was going on in the agricultural papers, as to the possibility of growing alfalfa in the dairy districts of New York. I studied the subject and planted a small area in May of the following year, only to meet with failure. Again I tried it, sowing as before about the middle of May — as I had been told to do by those who thought they knew — only to fail again. Had I used my reason I should have known better, since the best time for sowing other kinds of clover was from a month to six weeks earlier. For the third time, a quarter of an acre of alfalfa was sown; but for convenience sake and by mere chance, it was put in about the first

---

* See frontispiece in "The Cereals of America," by Thomas F. Hunt, Professor of Agronomy at Cornell University.

of April, and at last came success and added knowledge.

The following spring half of the field was sown as early as March and was well up when a late frost came. According to the authors I had read, it should have been destroyed, but while the red clover was nipped a little, the alfalfa was uninjured. How slow we are to discover such simple facts! The rest of the field was sown the next year, and this alfalfa was still making a record when it was plowed up a year or two ago. Professor Stone in a letter from Cornell, dated February 5, 1910, writes:

" The old alfalfa field has been plowed up to make room for plant gardens. Alfalfa was very successful there for several seasons and we got five or six tons of hay per acre from the tract."

All these fields that I have been describing, are now given over to the Athletic Association. A correspondent informs me that there has been expended up to June, 1909, in grading, draining, seeding and preparation, over thirty-seven thousand dollars. And it is reported that a fund of one hundred thousand dollars is to be raised for further improvements, mostly for buildings for the accommodation of the athletic teams and a stadium. It is expected that eventually a much larger sum will be expended in putting up a gymnasium with its various appurtenances. I am wondering if all this will result in making two " Young Blades " grow where it was so difficult for me to make one blade of corn grow, thirty-five years ago.

As the farm was already committed to an all-year-round dairy, I determined to raise mangel wurtzels, a large kind of beet, for the dairy cattle. Like other farmers at that time I planted them after the corn was planted, it being a major crop while the minor crop of roots could wait. While watching the men at the hateful task of weeding them, I endeavored to think of some plan by which the labor of tillage and weeding could be lessened and the cost of production as well. My first thought was that a summer fallow the previous year would reduce the weed growth; but that ran counter to my accepted theory that as far as possible, the ground should be occupied by plants the entire year, thus imitating Nature's modes of action. Nature grows a plant on every inch of arable land, thus furnishing food for millions of animals, while at the same time the soil grows more productive year by year. The three golden links, I used to say, were: to raise a plant to feed

7

an animal, to furnish fertility to raise another plant, to feed another animal to make more fertility; the farmer to take his toll as the links revolved.

While meditating on this matter of raising beets, the thought came to me: how did my father raise those fine beets in chopping the tops of which I cut off my sister's index finger? Then I remembered that as early as he could get the ground in good condition he always planted onions, peas, beets and other frost-resisting plants. So next spring I planted mangel wurtzels in April. The seeds germinated better than before and the beets got a good start before the warm weather germinated the weed seeds. This simple knowledge which had come down to me from a former generation, reduced the cost of raising mangolds below five cents — even as low as three cents per bushel, occasionally — thus making their cost as well as their feeding value compare favorably with other cattle foods. It was in such simple and accidental ways that the agricultural pioneers blazed the way before experiment stations were established.

I purposely over-stocked the farm in order to have an abundant supply of barn manure to restore the productivity of the depleted soil. But at first manures had to be hauled from the city, four hundred feet below, and that was not only up-hill business but resulted in seeding the farm with every noxious weed known in the locality and these gave us much hard work afterward to eradicate. In order to make up the annual shortage of food for the livestock I was compelled to rent some adjoining land; and it is only now, after more than thirty years, that the necessity for supplementing the eighty acres of arable land comprising the University Farm, has been met by the purchase of eight hundred and thirty-eight adjoining acres.

During all this early period I kept in mind the two objects for which the University Farm should be maintained: it was not only to be a model farm, it was to serve as a practical laboratory for investigation and instruction. It must therefore be large and varied enough to provide the broadest view of agricultural practice. As I now survey the agricultural colleges after a full generation of experimentation, I am struck by the fact that those which have farms of considerable size (less than half a score) and which have made the most extensive use of them as an educational equipment, are now the leaders in the promotion of scientific, practical and

profitable husbandry; while those which have
laid greater stress on classroom work than on
farm demonstration have fallen behind. Farming
in the classroom is too much like farming in the
city — it lacks the flavor of the soil. Not that I
prize scientific teaching less but proofs in the fields
and barns more. An agricultural college where
the farm is left out is like an old mowing-machine
that a farmer was tinkering by the roadside fence.
When a chauffeur stopped his automobile near by,
the farmer asked "What kind of a machine is
that?" "An automobile," the chauffeur replied,
"What kind of machine is yours?" "Ought-to-
mow-grass, but it won't," said the farmer.

The surprising thing about the back-to-the-farm
movement is, that it is fostered largely by city men.
The College President now talks flowingly and
learnedly about the "educational" farm, about
the dignity and nobility and independence of farm
life, and even tells the rising generation how he
used to shear sheep, mow grass and do other farm
stunts — all this to stiffen the student's vertebrae.
And the Professors of Greek listen approvingly
and exclaim, "Me too!" They have not the sin-
cerity or the courage to admit that farming is in
fact a strenuous occupation and that they themselves dodged it and chose the direction of soft

hands and a higher remuneration; nor would they acknowledge that since they made their choice they have seldom pined for the sound of the cowbell, the bleating of those lovely lambs or the raucous refrain of long-nosed, hungry Jersey Red pigs.

"They might mow grass but they won't!"

The students in agriculture being few, the farm was of necessity my chief reliance in building up the reputation of the department and I determined that it should be creditable to the University. At that time the Trustees had not much interest in the farm and did not know enough about it to appreciate my difficulties. Many years afterwards, before my connection with the University ceased, a Trustee was appointed to look over the farm and make a report upon it. The report was honest, thorough and highly commendatory and so at last after twenty-five years, my work received the recognition which its difficulties deserved. But during all that intermediate time, the business men who principally constituted the Board of Trustees did not realize its importance nor the stupendous results which were certain to come from intelligent effort. Of necessity the initial undertakings were very small; and the Agricultural Department shared the contempt heaped upon the University

as a "freshwater," "hayseed" affair. It was at
first far easier to convince the farmers that the
department was capable of becoming a great factor
in the uplift of their calling, than to gain the interest of the Trustees. But the history of the last
ten years shows that at last they have realized the
value of the College of Agriculture to the welfare
of the people of the rural districts as well as to
the cause of education.

FARM BUILDINGS

When I went to Cornell the farm buildings consisted of a small, dilapidated farm house and several low, rambling barns, useful in a way and not
altogether bad, which stood close to the college
buildings not far from the Gorge. I spent a
month's rent in advance in making the house habitable and then we moved in. About a year later
when I had definitely decided to remain at Cornell, I drew from a western investment which was
bringing ten per cent interest, eleven hundred dollars with which I installed modern sanitary con-
veniences and put this house in decent condition.
The University authorities agreed to charge off as
rent each year a stipulated amount until the total
sum should equal the amount advanced less the

interest. While the house was being repaired in a summer vacation, we lived in the classrooms in Morrill Hall. About a year later in this re-modelled house my youngest son, Roger Marr Roberts, was born on July 12, 1876. For the sake of finishing what I have to say about my dwellings, I may add that in 1877–78 I built a comfortable house on East Avenue, which is now owned and occupied by one of my former students, Professor Stocking of the Dairy Department.

When I took charge of the farm there was no provision for the farm hands; they had to live either in the town of Ithaca or the little village now called Forest Home, in either case far from their work. They sometimes drank too much and were tired out in climbing the hill before the day's work began, for at this time there was, of course, no street car to the Campus. It was imperative that they should live near their work so I began by having an old carpenter shop which stood near the barns, repaired and into it the dairyman and his family moved. Hard by stood a small building which Dr. Law had used when dissecting horses, and which had been abandoned because someone who lived near by objected to the use made of it. This little veterinary laboratory was moved away into an orchard where it was less conspicuous and when repaired and enlarged the families of two Danish workmen occupied it and immediately began to take in boarders and washing. Eight years later these two thrifty farmhands moved west, each of them taking with him about twelve hundred dollars.

The next year I invested some seven hundred and fifty dollars in a rent cottage for workmen, which I located near the old McCandless barn on the south side of the farm southeast of the present site of Sage College, in order to protect the barn from tramps and fire. I should have known better for it was one of the best things that ever happened when that monstrous building burned down a few years afterward. After the new barn (1881) which I shall describe in detail farther on, was erected, I invested a thousand dollars of my own money to provide a house for the foreman of the farm. After some years the University authorities took over these tenant houses which I had built at prices which let me out nearly even on cost but gave me little interest on the money. As I have already suggested, the housing of the workmen near their work and my interest in their welfare, resulted in making them more efficient and improving their habits.

MODEL BARN

Built under Professor Roberts direction, 1881; torn down
to make way for College buildings, 1912.

About a year after I came to Cornell the President asked me if I would not like to have a new
barn.   I said I was not ready for that; I did not
want to duplicate the mistakes of my predecessor
and I was not yet sure what branches of farm
activities should be most emphasized.   It was not
until 1880 that the " model barn" was erected;
by that time the University authorities had become
very anxious to get the old barn removed from
the Campus and so their response to my request
for a new barn was prompt and cordial.   The
Building Committee of the Trustees located it, but
after that they left me to plan and build it according to my own judgment.

The barn was an L-shaped structure and, as I
remember, 128 feet long and 120 feet broad —
when the piggery was added later, 140 feet broad
— and like the Dutchman's horse, "the biggest
the way you measured it last."   The lower story
was devoted to the dairy animals and from their
feet to the top of the metal cow surmounting the
lightning rod which projected about four feet
above the cupola, was just one hundred feet.   The
basement also contained a covered yard, an engine
and boiler, an ice house, a root cellar and a milk
delivery room.   The horses, wagons, granaries

and office occupied most of the second floor; the
sheep, grain, hay, straw and stationary thresher,
the third floor. The mows would hold the sheaves
of 600 to 700 bushels of grain and 100 tons of
hay. Provision was made for everything a barn
should contain except poultry — which it should
not contain.

President Adams, our second President, once
said when admiring the barn from that delightful
view from the reservoir, " The lines of that barn
are the most harmonious of any building on the
grounds." Later an addition was made to it
which injured its architectural beauty. To me it
was not only beautiful on the outside, but physically restful and mentally satisfying on the inside,
because it was the embodiment of my dreams.
This barn cost about $7,000 and the lumber, when
it was finally torn down in 1912 to make room for
an Agricultural College building, was estimated
to be worth about $4,000; and now another has
been erected way back on the farm which cost
nearly four times as much.

In the basement and under the horse stalls, a
space, about 44 by 60 feet, was set apart to store
manures, and this provided a place where the cows
might stretch their legs as health demanded. The

large crops of grain furnished straw enough to keep this exercising yard fairly tidy. I had a good deal of doubt about the advisability of such a yard, for someone had stated in one of the agricultural journals that the health of the cattle in it and especially of the horses over it would be greatly endangered by bacteria and by the gases. As a precaution I had the floors of the horse stables above this yard made practically water tight and gas-proof by using asphalt and tarred paper liberally between two layers of the double floor.

It is almost funny now to think how excessive this precaution was. When Professor Raymond Pearson — one of my former students, in 1911 Commissioner of Agriculture for New York, and now President of the Iowa State College of Agriculture and Mechanics Arts — was selected to be the head of the Dairy Department, he placed double doors between the cow stable and the milk receiving room, thereby forming a vestibule to keep the microbes from passing from the stable to the milk receiving room. Upon making a comparative test of the air in this fortified milk room and in the covered barn yard, by exposing petra plates, it was found that the air in the covered yard was distinctly freer from bacteria than the milk room.

The sheep quarters on the third floor, where winter lambs were reared, was practically frost proof. The lambs which yeaned in December and January were highly fed and, when from six to seven weeks old, were hog-dressed and expressed to New York City where they found a market at prices ranging from five to ten dollars per head. We learned among many other things, for this was an experimental as well as a commercial undertaking, that if the ewes were not shorn before going into winter quarters, the high feeding and mild temperature made it very uncomfortable for them, although such conditions were ideal for making the lambs grow rapidly. I may as well mention briefly here my only attempt to establish a flock of superior fine-wool American Merinos for instructional purposes. About the time this barn was built I bought thirty fine-wool sheep, paying for them about twice the ordinary price. The dogs chased several of them over a precipice, wounded others and practically destroyed the usefulness of the flock for the purposes for which I had designed them and so ended that experiment.

EXPERIMENTS IN SILAGE

About the time the barn was built there was a
good deal of talk in the farm journals as to the
desirability of preserving in silos or pits, green
roughage for livestock. I think only one permanent silo had then been built in America, though
many notions as to how they should be built were
paraded in the press. In order to try it out we
built in an angle of the barn a great cavernous silo
of concrete with a provision for two huge screws
by which silage could be pressed down solidly.
As the pressure was not a following one, the screw
had to be turned several times a day to serve its
purpose. This contrivance not being altogether
satisfactory, next year the material was weighted
with several tons of stone which worked better but
still did not meet my requirements. Then the
silage was weighted with a covering of two feet
of earth by which we hoped to form an air-tight
seal as well as attain a following pressure. But the
earth covering dried out rapidly, became porous,
and was scarcely better than the stones. Next
straw, kept thoroughly wet, was used as a covering; while it did not weight down the silage and
speedily became half-rotten, it proved to be the

best seal we had yet found. Now, I believe, the common practice is to keep the top of the silage quite moist which forms a seal of semi-decayed material two to four inches thick which is discarded when the silo is opened.

However, I was not yet content, for the silage was at one time too acid and others too dry and fire-fanged at the walls of the structure. So I constructed a cistern, of about seven tons capacity, the walls of which were asphalted to make them air-tight. When this was filled with roughage, burning charcoal in a kettle was put into the top of the silo and then the cover, which I had tried to make air-tight, was put in place and overlaid with about two feet of earth. This did not prove enough better than the open method to justify the large expense and the inconvenience in emptying the silo. Next, I had made a galvanized iron cylinder of five hundred to one thousand pounds capacity, which would at least be air-tight, and I filled it up with green corn. Then procuring two cylinders of compressed carbonic acid gas, the air in the little iron silo was forced out by forcing the carbonic acid gas in — the silo was thus filled with green corn and a deadly gas. I had succeeded at last for when the material came out it was apparently in just the same state as when it went in.

I sent a sample to Professor Henry of Wisconsin University and he wrote laconically: "You can't do it again!" But although I could and did, I saw that the expense of this method also was prohibitive.

LIVESTOCK

Without consulting the University authorities I gradually got rid of the miserable milch cows and other poor cattle which were on the farm when I took charge, and by the time the Universal Barn was built I was beginning to build up a creditable herd; but I was not yet out of trouble. A wealthy tea merchant of New York City, who was a breeder of fancy Jersey cattle, and a friend of one of the Trustees, donated to the farm two cows, and a bull was purchased from him at a nominal price. At this time Jerseys were believed to be the best of all dairy breeds.

Meanwhile, I had become interested in Holsteins. Mr. W. W. Chenery of Boston, on a business trip to the Netherlands, had admired and purchased a cow of one of the now well-known Holstein-Friesian breed of dairy cattle, which proved to be so satisfactory that he soon imported a male and some more females and established a small herd in the suburbs of Boston — the first one of this breed in this country. By reading the current livestock literature I had become familiar with this venture. I had already learned, by keeping detailed accounts of the various sub-divisions of the farm activities such as dairy, workstock, wheat, oats, hay and the like, that the dairy was the most satisfactory pot-boiler of them all. Having obtained permission from the University authorities to buy some of this breed I purchased from Mr. Chenery two full-bloods and one half-blood — all that my money would buy.

For many years Ezra Cornell had maintained on his farm adjoining the College grounds a fine herd of Shorthorns and just as I was congratulating myself on having made a start in two good dairy breeds, there came through a second person and like a clap of thunder from a clear sky, a serious objection. The Governor of the State was the son of our honored founder and it seemed that he thought that the bringing of those black and white cattle to the College Farm had greatly depreciated the value of his father's holdings. It must be explained that although the Shorthorns were regarded as the beef breed, *par excellence,* certain strains or families of them as for instance the Princess tribe, were considered excellent dairy animals. In 1873, the Eighth Duchess of Geneva had sold at public auction at New York Mills, for forty thousand six hundred dollars and other animals of the same blood for nearly as much. It was quite natural that Mr. Cornell's son should speak slightingly of my purchase and I felt that it was most unfortunate that I had offended so influential a man. The thing was done, however, and there was nothing that could palliate it.

Soon afterwards I was diverted by a far more serious trouble; some of my cherished pure-blood animals contracted tuberculosis, probably from germs lurking in the old stables, for thorough disinfection had not been thought of at that time. With the aid of Dr. Law the battle against it was carried on and when the cattle were moved to the Universal Barn we supposed it was eradicated — but we were mistaken. Tuberculin had not yet been used for discovering incipient tuberculosis and it was a long time before we finally had a clean herd. During all this time very little progress could be made in improving the milk-producing power of the herd and in ten years little had been accomplished toward establishing a herd worthy of an agricultural college.

I can scarcely expect the reader of these small beginnings and of all these troubles to understand

how important they were to me. To displease the
son of the truly great man who had given his life
and fortune to Cornell University was a grief to
me and scarcely less to offend the Governor of the
State. Some of my mistakes I now attribute to the
fact that I was too secretive and had no intimate
friend with whom I could take counsel; but some
of them were due to pioneer conditions and must
have been made by any teacher of agriculture.
And through it all for many years I felt that the
College of Agriculture existed only by sufferance
and that I had no real sympathy or cooperation
from the Trustees. I sometimes wonder now why
I struggled on — why I did not quit the job; and I
can only suppose that it was because the dream of
what might be done still lured me on.

I believed that if I won out at all it must be by
doing something for the State which others had
not been able to do. The University needed a
large and highly productive dairy not only to educate the students but to educate the dairymen of
the State so that they would improve their dairies,
for milk production was one of the foremost of
its industries. Year after year I quietly picked up
a Jersey here and a Holstein there, bred grades
and a few pure-bloods, sold every season the

poorest of the herd — as many as nine at one time — replacing them by purchases of better ones or by those of our own raising; until the dairy herd of twenty-five cows averaged — including two-year old heifers which should have been counted as half cows — eight thousand pounds per cow per year. Some of the best cows exceeded twelve thousand pounds per year. At that time the State Dairymen's Association estimated that the average yield per cow per year throughout the State was between three thousand and three thousand five hundred pounds. So at last the stars in the " Milky " way shone clear above the Cornell hills.

About 1885 Professor H. H. Wing became my assistant and some years later took entire charge of the Dairy Department. But once more we had a scare on account of tuberculosis. Once a year the herd was tested with tuberculin, and that year a fine Holstein bull responded to the test. It was hard to believe it and a second test was made which confirmed the first. To improve the dairy cattle of the surrounding country I had offered the services of this bull to the farmers at a nominal price and they had availed themselves of the offer. Dr. Law afterward concluded that the bull had become infected from this outside source for, when he was killed, the herd remained clean.

HORTICULTURE

When I began at Cornell in 1874, Professor A. N. Prentiss occupied the Chair of Botany and Horticulture. His classes in Botany were always very large as it was a required study in several of the general courses. He had inadequate assistance, for it was difficult in these earlier years for the University to get funds even for running expenses. Consequently little could be done to give the students a knowledge of the simplest principles of horticulture, though botany was well taught. As both of these branches were fundamental to any broad conception of agricultural education, I was anxious to enlarge the work to include training in practical horticulture and pomology; and all the more as New York was then a leading state in fruit culture.

I asked for an instructor in pomology and horticulture and the Trustees appointed Mr. W. R. Lazenby — a recent graduate of the Department — to that position. He started out in a very simple and economical way, endeavoring to use the land assigned to him for gardens as a working laboratory and to pay expenses as well. Even under the management of a more experienced man this would have been an impossibility for the University gardens were located four hundred feet above the valley and the crops could not be ready to harvest until at least two weeks after those grown below. By the time our products were put on the market it was glutted and prices were below the cost of production.

Mr. Lazenby also labored under other difficulties in that Professor Prentiss was overworked and in delicate health and had not time or strength to guide his young assistant. The fates being against us altogether, the attempt was abandoned.

Several years afterwards it became evident that the Department must be re-established and when asked by one of the Trustees as to the best man to put in charge I said that I knew of only one who would be certain to make a success of the undertaking — Professor Liberty Hyde Bailey, then at Michigan Agricultural College. As to means I thought the Trustees should be prepared to furnish enough to give the Department a fair start; and as to the details, the Professor appointed should be free to work them out to suit the local environment and in accordance with his own judgment. Professor Bailey was selected to take charge of this Department which was then separated from

Botany. It is superfluous for me to recount here the story of his great success.

The Trustees made a liberal appropriation for this Department and when the United States Experiment Station funds were yearly apportioned among the various investigational divisions, I invariably recommended that the horticultural division should receive the largest share, since it had suffered long years of arrested development. So with an able man at the head and with good resources — considering the demands of other interests — the Department grew by leaps and bounds. And I am proud of the fact that I was instrumental in influencing the Trustees to furnish the means and to appoint the man who so wonderfully carried out the task.

THE CHICKEN BUSINESS (which deserves a chapter all by itself !)

About 1888 a smiling young student approached me and asked me why we didn't have a poultry department? I replied rather sharply that I knew nothing about the chicken business; had no means to employ a man who did, if there was such a man; and that I had seen so many persons go through the chicken fever and come out looking like a moulting hen sitting on one egg, that I was in a critical frame of mind. Without being daunted in the least, he said that he knew something about the chicken business and would like to try his hand at it. He thought poultry culture ought to be taught at the college and he proceeded to describe enthusiastically, ways, means and possible results.

He finally got me interested and I told him to draw up plans for a poultry plant. When he brought them to me I thought them quite too elaborate and so, turning over his paper, I sketched on the back four lines enclosing a space of about twelve by twenty feet. I proposed that with our own hands we should build the first chicken house out of a great pile of refuse lumber left from an old barn; that we should locate it some distance away from the other buildings at the edge of a little wood. I warned him furthermore that if he let that poultry house become disreputable, like many I had seen, I would turn out the hens and burn it down, lice and all.

I worked with him until the building was enclosed and then told him to put in any kind of chicken fixings he liked and if at first they didn't suit, tear them out as often as he pleased, for the lumber he would destroy was worth nothing to speak of. The boy experimented on himself and the chickens during the remainder of his college course and then went into business for himself. Later someone discovered that that enthusiastic Cornell graduate knew a lot about poultry and had a faculty of stating so clearly and forcibly what he knew that he could convince others. And thus it was that Mr. James Rice came to be much sought after as a travelling instructor by the Farmer's Institute management.

Some time afterwards, Mr. George Watson — author of *Farm Poultry* (1901) — who was also a graduate of the University, was employed to assist me in experimental work and to take charge of the poultry. The work went on so satisfactorily that the experimental industry had to be enlarged by building another house out of the refuse pile. As students increased other colony houses were built, one each year, until there were half a dozen or more, the construction work being done largely by students in the regular hours arranged for farm practice. It was while the students, Mr. Watson and I were building the third house, I think, that the chairman of the Executive Committee drove up one afternoon, glanced at us, and turned and drove away without so much as passing the time of day. As it was the first time I had ever seen him on the agricultural part of the farm, I was very much disturbed, for I had not asked either for permission to build nor an appropriation to run, a poultry plant. The fact was, the College was growing so slowly that I determined to risk something to develop this branch since it would cost so little. My anxiety was wasted, however, for he never took any notice of the matter.

Personally I had little to do with the Poultry Department except to give it general direction and to squeeze the inadequate farm appropriation enough each year to make it hatch a modest chicken house until we had built seven of them. I do take credit, however, for furnishing that zealous Sophomore with his opportunity and with teaching him to begin experiments on a small scale. I am delighted to learn that the desire for instruction in poultry husbandry has so far outrun the facilities that a new and larger plant is urgently required and is likely to be supplied in the near future. I have just read that bills have been introduced simultaneously into both houses of the New York Legislature to appropriate $90,000 for the construction and equipment of a poultry husbandry building. According to the latest report that I have by me (1910), James Rice is now the head of the Poultry Department at Cornell and has 167 students under him. So much can enthusiasm and energy do in one line of agriculture.

EXPERIMENTATION AND INVESTIGATION

About 1883 — I cannot fix the exact date — a meeting was called by President White to discuss the subject of establishing an agricultural experiment station at Cornell. There were present, as I now recall, the President, the Honorable J. Stanton Gould, Professor G. C. Caldwell, and myself. As a result of this meeting a bill was drawn up, soon afterwards passed in the State Legislature without opposition, signed by Governor Cornell, and became a law. The bill provided that the Legislature should appoint three men to decide upon the most favorable location for the station. Before we at Cornell had a hint of what was being done, the Legislative Committee selected a farm near Geneva, at the foot of Seneca Lake, and reported back to the Legislature, which approved the report. It was a sharp political move: two of the committeemen were enemies of Cornell and the third was a man easily influenced. The Governor always blamed us, and justly, I think, for not watching the appointment of the committee closely enough, but I doubt if any amount of watching would have secured the Station for Cornell University. We had not enough political influence at that time to dictate who should be appointed on the committee. We should have foreseen perhaps, what would be likely to happen and have given the Governor a tip so that he would not sign the bill.

But all's well that ends well; and time has shown that there is ample room in so large, populous and diversified a State as New York for two stations. I am now inclined to think that if it had been located at Cornell the station might have brought upon us more criticism than the University already suffered. Because the College was not administered by some religious denomination and because the President had selected a corps of scientific lecturers and professors who valued truth more than legend, the churches were violently antagonistic. When the Press announced one fall that a large number — 300, I think — had entered the Freshman class, a leading denominational journal declared that 300 " fresh recruits for Satan " had entered this " Godless college." Another journal called it "a school where hayseeds and greasy mechanics were taught to hoe potatoes, pitch manure and be dry nurses to steam engines." We were even dubbed a "Godless, fresh-water college planted in Ezra Cornell's potato patch," by the students of one of the older New England Colleges. These and many other things of the same sort were hard to bear, for at that time we were not sure that we should laugh last.

Although we had lost the experiment station we went on with research work and published our results in three good-sized bulletins (1879–1885), the expense of printing being borne by that generous and sympathetic woman, the late Jennie McGraw-Fiske, who was deeply concerned with the welfare of the University.

THE FEDERAL EXPERIMENT STATION AT CORNELL

In March, 1887, Congress passed a general act establishing agricultural experiment stations throughout the country. This act provided $15,000 annually for each State and Territory with which to conduct investigations in agriculture and to publish a detailed report of them. The first question to be solved in most of the States was whether it was best to merge the station in the agricultural college or to establish a distinct organization not vitally connected with it. At Cornell it was agreed that no vigorous experimental department could be established and maintained on an annual income of $15,000 without the aid of the College staff and the use of its equipment. So the Federal Station was made a part of the Agricultural College.

As to the directorship of the Station, President Adams agreed with me that this heavy duty should not be added to the varied responsibilities I already had and he therefore recommended that a director should be appointed who should give all his time to investigation; and that the assistant investigators should also be instructors, giving, for economy's sake, a part of their time to college work and a part to research. The Executive Committee of the Board of Trustees agreed with us at first and appointed Major E. A. Alvord director of the Station, who declined the position.

After searching the country over for another available candidate, President Adams recommended me for the office and the Executive Committee appointed me. I declined at first to accept these additional duties; and Mr. Henry W. Sage,

the Chairman, told me I was making the mistake
of my life. Finally and with great reluctance, I
accepted the position for that year. But Mr.
Sage was right, for two directors could not very
long have coöperated peacefully in using the same
plant and in employing the same men to conduct
investigations under one chief and to give instruction under another — any more than two queen
bees can remain long in the same hive. So, again,
to return to my old metaphor, I was saved by
President Adams and Mr. Sage from a head-on
collision.

As I remember it, I was made Director in May
and if we did not use the first appropriation by
June 30th of the current year, it would lapse into
the Treasury of the United States. To invest so
large an amount judiciously in a technical equipment was no easy task. There were all sorts of
things to be purchased, some in foreign countries,
and the bills must be viséd by the Director and approved by the Executive Committee by the last
day of June. Professor Comstock made his plans
for an Insectary — the first ever built — between
two days, I think, and got his bills in on time.
One of our Professors who was then in Europe
was instructed by cablegram to buy certain appliances which could not be had at home, and the

bills arrived in time to be included in the budget, although the articles did not come till later.

You would naturally think that when this first appropriation was expended in appliances the rush would be over; but the Congressional Act provided that an annual report must be made which must contain not only an itemized account of expenditures and receipts but also a report of the progress of the work in hand. I turned, therefore, to material on hand which had not yet been published in the bulletins previously mentioned. This and some other research stuff that we had in hand was prepared for publication and handed to the President. I told him that I knew absolutely nothing about matters of printing and publication and he advised me to put the matter in the hands of Mr. Church, one of the members of the publishing firm of Andrus & Church, in Ithaca, who had good taste in such matters. I did so, giving him no other directions than that the report must be a first-class job all round. In the subsequent bulletins these requirements have held good through all the years and their general appearance remains much the same as at the beginning. Up to 1903, the date of my retirement, there had been published by the Experiment Station fifteen

Annual Reports, comprising 6,326 pages of printed matter. As I look back over them, they testify to the success which the Station met with from the first. Although at the end of the first year I gave in my resignation, the President told me that the Trustees were more than satisfied and that they hoped the question of a Director would not again be raised. Thus I became the permanent head of it, a position which I retained until my departure from the University.

It was not customary to embody an account of our failures in these reports but one of them may be worth recording here. As I have stated before, Dr. Law and I made several attempts to eradicate tuberculosis from the dairy herd. The disease was very imperfectly understood at that time, so I offered to build a small, sanitary stable at some distance from other buildings, in which to conduct experiments in bovine tuberculosis.

I had seen for the first time while on a visit to a large potato raiser, Mr. T. B. Terry of Ohio, large hollow vitrified bricks. They were about eight inches square and perhaps two feet long, and I thought they would exactly suit my purpose. So a carload of them was ordered and with them the erection of a double-compartment stable was be-

gun. When it was just about ready for the roof
timbers, President White stopped the building
because he feared that the flies from this veterinary
laboratory would reach his barn and house and
carry the germs of this dreaded disease with them.
So this second attempt to build a veterinary laboratory came to naught and after a year or two Professor Bailey tore it down and used those hollow
bricks, on which I had counted so much, as foundation material for his forcing houses. It is amusing to remember in this connection that the large
buildings of the Veterinary College were later
placed as close to the President's house on
the south as my little veterinary house had been
on the east — and thereby hangs a tale — but it is
not for me to tell!

It was our custom to conduct simple investigations away from the College on the farms of men
who were willing to coöperate with us, and an extensive experiment in sugar-beet culture was so
conducted under a State appropriation. Some parties in Binghamton became interested in beet culture and as there were no data at that time as to
yield or quality of beets raised in New York, we
gladly took up this line of investigation. For three
consecutive years we procured seeds of improved

8

varieties, mailed them with full printed directions as to culture, harvesting and recording of facts, to one or two hundred farmers whom we had interested in the work. Each year we had from two to five hundred samples of beets to analyze. At the end of the first year a beet-sugar company was formed at Binghamton, works were erected and equipped and after the harvest of the second season of our experiments, I had the pleasure of taking my class to the works to see the first sugar ever made from beets — in a large way — in the State of New York.

While the land about Binghamton produced beets of a high sugar content, it was not such as to make beet growing profitable, much of it being too clayey or too stoney; it was difficult to get enough cheap foreign labor — for the American does not take kindly to farming on his knees in weeding and harvest time. For this and other reasons the factory was afterward moved to one of the western States. But our labor was not in vain for it furnished valuable information not only to the farmers but to the Station staff, while putting us in friendly communication with the most progressive farmers of that portion of the State.

THE STATE EXPERIMENT STATION AT GENEVA

When the Federal Experiment Station was established at Cornell only forty miles from the State Station at Geneva, it was naturally supposed that there would be some friction between them. Dr. E. L. Sturtevant was chosen to be the first Director of the Geneva Station and as he was a reasonable and at the same time, liberal-minded man, our relations during his incumbency were most friendly, in spite of the antagonism of some of the members of his Board of Control who threatened to absorb us. The second Director of the Geneva Station was Dr. Jacob Collier, who had attracted some notice by his advocacy of the establishment of a factory for manufacturing sugar from the sorghum plant (*andropogan sorghum*). He certainly did much valuable chemical work along this line and became so enthusiastic over it — so I have been told — that the Board of Control at Geneva exacted a promise from him that he would dismount from his hobby if he was chosen Director of the Station.

I had been in the habit of taking my class to inspect the work of this Station once or twice a year, but soon after Dr. Collier took charge the

practice was given up as the Station atmosphere
had become unfriendly. When it became evident
that Dr. Collier would have to give up his place
because of failing health, I was invited to succeed
him. The outlook at Cornell was very discourag-
ing at this time and I presume I had expressed my
dissatisfaction to someone in an unguarded
moment. At any rate two members of the Board
of Control at Geneva made me a visit and urged
me to accept the State Directorship, promising
everything that could reasonably be expected. I
confess I was greatly tempted to resign from Cornell but I finally decided to decline the offer because I felt that I had started out to attain one
great object — the laying of the foundations of a
great agricultural college — and that to abandon
it because it was more difficult than I had antici-
pated, would be cowardly.

Dr. William H. Jordan was then appointed
Director and a most fortunate selection it was.
On taking charge he found, hidden away in a
closet, copies of a little circular containing an at-
tack on the Federal Station and the College of
Agriculture at Cornell which, for some unex-
plained reason, had not been sent out. After this
I had but one serious contention with the Geneva

Station and that arose when the State Station made a demand for a part of our annual Federal appropriation of $15,000 in order that the State Station might secure thereby, the franking privilege for their bulletins. The matter was finally amicably adjusted by a legal enactment which gave to the State Station 10 per cent. of our appropriation — fifteen hundred dollars annually — thus permitting it to send out printed mail free of postage.

AGRICULTURAL EDUCATION

In the seventies it was generally believed that an agricultural college could not be successfully grafted on to a university and the evidence seemed to prove it; but when I looked at all sides of the question I was convinced that a college of agriculture could never take a dignified place in the world of higher education unless its entrance requirements and its courses of study were made equal in length and in severity — though not necessarily the same in kind — to those prevailing in the colleges of Science and of the Arts. As yet the agricultural colleges made no such requirements and were not likely to for many years to come.

I did not then fully realize the difficult position in which the first graduates of the colleges were placed. The farmers and the legislators who voted appropriations called loudly for these colleges to turn out educated farmers at a time when any tyro with a little capital could go west and, by gently tickling the rich, virgin prairies, secure an abundant harvest without any education whatever. The agricultural graduate was, therefore, usually compelled to find employment in some other field or else compete with unskilled labor. On the other hand, when the graduates of these colleges came in touch with the graduates of the colleges of Science and the Arts, they could but realize their lack of general culture as judged by the world's standards. Some of the more far-seeing graduates amplified their studies and in time reached positions of distinction, but I am sure that they regretted that the foundations of their education had not been laid deeper and broader. I could sympathize with them in their humiliation because I had toiled up by the same difficult way. All these things I began to realize dimly while I was trying to determine the direction which the agricultural courses should take in order to lay a foundation for the College at Cornell which should not be inferior in any respect — when suitably maintained — to any other in the Cornell group.

Almost from the first I desired a farm laboratory. In all of the technical departments of the University I saw men trying to learn how to do things by *doing* them. Although I had made from the first considerable use of portions of the small college farm for this purpose, the attempt to give students anything like skill or first-hand knowledge by illustrations on such restricted space, was most unsatisfactory. Three times I secured options on adjacent farms and recommended their purchase to the Trustees — only to meet with refusal. The Board had to be differently constituted before more land would be granted for strictly educational purposes.

At one time I nearly completed an arrangement with a neighboring farmer who was childless, to give the use of his farm to the College, the University agreeing to pay a stipulated rental for it as long as he or his wife should live. At their death the farm was to go to the University as a gift. On this occasion my hopes ran high, for here on this farm — which had two sizable houses on it — I could carry out my cherished plans. I intended to arrange the courses of study so that the senior work at the College would be completed early in April, at which time the entire senior class would be taken to the farm, together with a suitable number of instructors in farm practice, and a few domestics to care for the farm houses where they would live. Here with a small dairy, tools, implements and workstock, the ordinary farm operations (except the harvesting of corn, wheat, etc.) could be carried on in a practical, systematic way. The students could be required to do continuous, productive labor long enough to learn the meaning of a day's work. I believed that this sort of training would greatly improve their judgment and would give them a better hold on the complexities and difficulties of farm life.

But all this came to naught because I could not convert the authorities to my scheme; and I was compelled to recommend for graduation for many years students who had no acquaintance whatever with farm practice. At the present time it is perfectly apparent that the technical departments throughout the country which have been able to give thorough training in *doing* things are overrun with students and have attained wide and deservedly high reputations. And yet, even now, in certain lines of agricultural instruction, almost no effort is being made to give students a working knowledge of the operations of the farm. Although agricultural students are now, in many cases, required to know the handicraft of farming when they enter college, they seldom have enough practical knowledge to enable them to assimilate the scientific training which they receive in College.

Eight years in the Primary and Grammar schools and four years in the High School are now required to fit pupils for the University and for the best agricultural colleges. Even if the boy is a farmer's son and has a disposition to learn manual things, there is not enough time left outside of school hours nor is the preparatory student mature enough to see their bearing upon the sciences which he is to study in college. Nature study may very properly be taught in the schools but not the farm handicrafts.

The agricultural colleges must take one of two courses: they must either require students to take practical examinations in farming before entering college or they must provide the means whereby they can acquire in college enough practical knowledge to save them from being the laughing stock of the unlettered farmer. The first seems to me undesirable even if the schools and the farmers together were willing to attempt it. There is, therefore, no way but to provide for this practical instruction in the college itself. It is unjust to the boy graduate of twenty-two and misleading to the public to give a college degree which predicates a knowledge of rural affairs, when the instructors all know that the first attempt that the student makes to embody his learning in visible, remunerative results, will almost certainly fail. Indeed, he may be so humiliated that his college enthusiasm and his ideals of a more intelligent rural life will be shattered and perhaps for life.

General agriculture is now the only subject in which students are not required to become fairly skillful before they are expected to take up its practice. The students of chemistry, of mechanic arts, of civil engineering, of the law — all do over and over again as nearly as possible the very things that they will have to do when they go out to take up their chosen calling. What use would a railway have for the graduate of a college of Civil Engineering who had not progressed farther along the applied side of his profession than to be able to carry a Gunter's chain? The railways demand men who can do things, real things that are too difficult for untrained men, and the stress is laid on the doing and not on the theory.

In like manner the landowner does not want an agricultural graduate who cannot harness a span of horses, plow a furrow, pack a barrel of apples or trim a tree correctly; nor one who hitches a driving horse to a post with the line without first taking it out of the turrets. Now that the agricultural colleges have grown relatively rich and strong and are no longer manned by pioneers but by able, trained and experienced instructors, it is little less than criminal to graduate students who are careless in the use of figures and words; who cannot make out a balance sheet embodying the results of the operations of a farm; who cannot dig a post hole in the right place nor dig it with the least possible labor nor set three posts in a line; nor bore a hole straight in a timber without a plumb-bob. Some men, I fear many, have been graduated, whom you would not trust to harrow the potato patch for fear they would ruin a span of horses by getting it on the harrow or by getting the harrow on top of the span.

The way to learn one part of agriculture, and a most important part, is to do agriculture. If students object to the toil of learning the fundamentals—without remuneration—then turn them out to grass and let them graze within the pasture of any other college which will adopt a maverick. Since coming to California I have seen two agricultural college graduates occupying honorable and responsible positions and otherwise able men in some directions, put to shame because they were deficient in the basic knowledge of their calling. In the early days, the agricultural students were generally directly from the farm and while the colleges were blazing the way there was nothing to do but wink at their deficiencies. Although I myself was one of the pioneers I did everything in my power to bridge the gap between practice and science but always came short of doing so, for one man cannot be all things to all men in agriculture any more than in other callings.

In some lines instruction has been greatly improved since my time; for instance, students in dairy husbandry learn how to make butter and cheese by making butter and cheese; they know when a can is clean by making it clean, while formerly we talked about dairying in the class-room. But in general the agricultural colleges are still reprehensibly negligent in allowing students to graduate who are top-heavy with science. For this lack of practical dexterity sometimes the excuse is made that four years at college is not sufficient time for students to acquire a moderate proficiency in those studies which are chiefly useful in training men to think deeply, logically and constructively and to express themselves clearly, much less to acquire practical dexterity. There is just enough of truth in this to mislead and its fallacy will be made clear in a later discussion of the courses of study.

More and more it is becoming apparent that there should be auxiliary agricultural schools of lower requirements than those which the colleges exact. Large numbers of young people are now desiring to study agriculture who have neither the inclination nor the time to take a four-year collegiate course. There is no provision for giving technical instruction in agriculture in the public schools and never should be; though there are many simple things which are most interesting and important to know, no matter what station pupils may afterward fill, and which should be taught in the public school. They might be called "kindergarten science" or, preferably, by that all-embracing and appropriate name already in use, "Nature study." Every American child has a right to good instruction along this line but to call this general nature-information, agriculture, is utterly misleading. The public school curriculum is already overloaded and agriculture proper has little to do with the lives of a majority of the pupils; but Nature study is a cultural study which develops the child's normal instinct to become acquainted with the objects by which it is surrounded.

As the schools are now conducted, the tendency is to stunt and suppress this fundamental characteristic of all healthy children. The complaint is frequently made that the schools educate children away from agriculture; the fact is, the tendency is to develop the conventional and the artificial instead of the fundamentally natural. Agriculture happens to suffer most because farming is a business that has most to do with the forces of nature which produce life and growth and indispensable commodities — a business founded on the sciences. For a long time there was a gap between the public schools and the colleges filled — in New York and in other of the older States — by academies of a high grade. The large number of private schools which prosper because they undertake to fit pupils for entrance to college, indicates that the gap has not been satisfactorily bridged by the public High School. Considered from the needs of the rural population, the gap is a chasm. Now the attempt is being made to organize the public schools so that there will be no gap between them and the colleges; and the auxiliary agricultural schools and the agricultural High School should close the gap between the public schools and the agricultural college. If agricultural schools, as many and as efficient as the old-fashioned academies, were scattered throughout the States, they would do much to solve many vexed country problems; for it would mean giving to the rural communities an opportunity to acquire such training of mind and hand as would fit them reasonably well for making the most of their resources.

In the earlier days there was no question as to accepting work done in the academies for entrance to the college, so far as it might go; but now all work completed in the High School is not accepted for entrance and a discrimination is made in the work of the different High Schools, some being accepted and some refused. This may be a cheap way to bring badly managed schools up to the standard but it is done at the expense of the prospective college student instead of the State. It should be the business of the State to bring the High Schools up to so nearly uniform a standard that those who present themselves at the college would stand on an equal footing, no matter from what school they come. As to private fitting schools, perhaps there is no better way than for the college to inspect them and then place them on the accepted or non-accepted list.

In such a system, the agricultural academies should be under the control of a Board composed of the faculty of the State Agricultural College and the principals of the agricultural schools; who should have the power to formulate rules for entrance, courses of study and practice and determine the kind and amount of work which would be received at the college towards fulfilling the requirements for entrance and for graduation. The academies might — I think should — require the payment of a small tuition fee; for if the academy lays as much stress on the art of farming as it should, it will be very expensive if the number of students is restricted as it should be.

The fact is, we are still laying the stress on numbers instead of on efficient instruction. "Walks and Talks," such as I gave forty years ago at the Iowa College and later at Cornell are useful but they are only second-hand work; and no teacher can successfully handle more than half a score of students at a time when it comes to teaching the art of farming, and one student may sometimes prove to be a large class.

I think too, that it will be found that most students would prefer to learn farming at an academy rather than at College and I am certain that it would be better for them to do so. Supposing a prospective college student is somewhat deficient in the entrance requirements; what better place than the agricultural academy in the quiet country in which to make up deficiencies and obtain a slight knowledge of farm practice? For the necessary subjects only a few teachers would be required in each academy. We already have many teachers who have experience and proved ability in our High Schools for every subject except agriculture — all that is needed is skill in selecting them and that should be found among the colleges.

I have just read an excellent address by President Raymond Pearson, of Iowa, given when he was President of the New York Agricultural Society and Commissioner of Agriculture; and I take the liberty of making quotations and discussing it because he was formerly one of my students and because he is a leader in agricultural progress. His clear insight is very refreshing:

"Our agricultural problem today is more than anything else a financial one. . . . The cheerless farm home is supposed by some to be the cause of lack of interest in country life, but it has been demonstrated in hundreds of homes that good cheer and abundant comforts in the form of improved houses with modern facilities, lawns, and even automobiles come quickly, when the farmers are financially successful."

Pointing out that the study of agriculture has become highly popular, he says:

"In this State there are at least twenty-one different kinds of agencies" (and two more to be added soon) "working for the advancement of agricultural interests, chiefly by making known better methods. . . . No two of these schools are alike either in details of schedules or management."

To a pioneer this alacrity to climb on the farmers' band-wagon is amusing. There are many who want to ride and are climbing in over the tailboard, now that the crop is ready to harvest. Professor Pearson goes on to say that there are in New York alone twenty institutions for agricultural promotion supported wholly or in part by the State, and two altogether supported by the Federal Government. This tremendous and expensive equipment is broken up into fragments and each is being used, largely irrespective of the others, to solve one of three greatest problems of the age.

And certainly of these three — War, Drunkenness and Bread — Bread is fundamentally most
important.

The inertia which had to be overcome in earlier
days has been transformed into resistless energy
and the time has come in New York to lay aside
all jealousies, all bickerings as to men and localities, that these fragmentary efforts may be coördinated; for if this is not speedily done, the attempt
to wrest support for all of them from the State
will create such antagonism as will destroy the
weaker ones and cause the stronger to spend their
energy chiefly in the political struggle for exist-
ence. In recent years at Albany there have been
signs that this destructive competition is only restrained by the wisdom of a few leaders.

Commissioner Pearson further says:

"The exceptional educational facilities (in New
York) including the common school system, are believed to be the best in the world."

But these schools of which New Yorkers are
justly proud, are not left to go as they please but
are carefully coördinated into one logical, symmetrical whole by a small body of able men. Until agricultural education is organized and directed
in a similar manner no one will be able to say that

the Empire State has the best system of agricultural education in the world. It should not be long
before that could be truthfully said of a State so
bountifully supplied with noble streams and
forests, arable soils and salubrious climate; and
with a population of intelligent people possessing
unbounded means for carrying on commerce,
manufacture and trade, and for producing the
great abundance of commodities which make them
possible.

Dean L. H. Bailey has said that practically half
of New York State is still in woods, swamps and
waste — a conservative estimate. Add to this the
possibility of doubling the yield per acre and we
have a possible output from rural endeavor only a
little short of $1,000,000,000 annually. And
this too, figured on the prices received and the
quantities of products produced as long ago as
1899. This work lies at the very door of the
agricultural college, the academies and the other
agencies mentioned by Professor Pearson. One
of the pioneers in agriculture has predicted, I believe, that it will not take more than fifty years to
reach the billion-dollar mark. In fifty years of
my life I have seen as great change and advancement in the means of communication and transpor-
tation, and in the comforts and luxuries of the

home, as will have to be made in the production of animals and plants to reach the mark which has been set above.

The farmers ask the trained experts to teach them how to make $2 drop into their pockets where only $1 dropped in 1899 — they want to take their turn at riding, for the men who ride have always led and ruled the world. So long as the world sat down to a good cheap breakfast, furnished by the farmer at less than the cost of production, it turned to the stock and bond sales and the reports of the clearing houses of the previous day for a measure of prosperity; now it turns to the provision column before taking another piece of bacon or asking for another egg. It is astonishing how many people have come to take a vital interest in the welfare of the farmer since he has attained a small bank account. Far be it from me, who was once one of them, to make light of this new-found interest. The prices of farm products which result in a fair wage for the farmer in some cases, and in a modest profit for a few will, if continued, do much to precipitate the solution of agricultural problems which have been waiting through the centuries.

I am writing this here in my little study in California on the twenty-fifth day of April amid a sea

of roses and in a land overflowing with plenty, so
I can't help being optimistic and perhaps just a
little flowery. When I compare present conditions
with some I have been through in the past I rejoice
with exceeding great joy. I am fully persuaded
that the many educational agencies which have
been at work during the last half century for the
help of the rural classes, have been major factors
in accomplishing the vast improvement in social
life and productive effort in the farming districts.
But there is much yet to be done so I am profoundly impressed with the need of using eco-
nomically and efficiently the agencies already established for the education of those who furnish food
for themselves and for the world. When that is
accomplished such other agencies as experience
proves to be needful may be added. The agricultural education which is founded on a knowledge
of conditions, on skill and upon the accumulated
literature of science, is only of yesterday and it
would be strange if we were not formulating some
schemes which will be greatly improved in the
future. I am sometimes called " a pioneer in agricultural education; " and therefore I may caution
those who are now in the field and at work, that I
left many invisible stones and roots in the soil

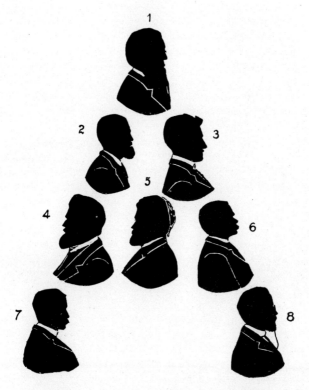

CORNELL FACULTY OF AGRICULTURE, 1891

Silhouettes on menu of first banquet of College of Agriculture. 1, Roberts; 2, Wing; 3, Bailey; 4, Law; 5, Caldwell; 6, Comstock; 7, Dudley; 8, Prentiss.

which may fetch them up standing as they plow deeper than I did.

EXPERIENCE WITH NEW YORK STATE ORGANIZATIONS

During the first year of my stay at Cornell I received an invitation to deliver an address before the State Dairymen's Association. Coming from the undeveloped prairies of Iowa and all untrained in public speaking, I realized that this would be a severe test of my fitness for my position. I supposed that the East was far in advance of the West so I selected a difficult and advanced subject — "The Conservation of Warmth in Dairy Barns." I tried to show how much more economical it was to conserve warmth by means of well-constructed stables than to produce it by expensive forage fed to the animals. I showed conclusively that the cow first used her food to maintain her bodily temperature and second, to replace worn-out tissues; and that it was only the surplus over these two needs which went into gain in weight or into the milk pail. I demonstrated that a good cow maintained her in-born motherly instinct often at the expense of her bodily weight in order to provide food for her young; but that the first toll of

the nutrition went to maintain bodily heat and if all
of the ration was consumed for this purpose there
were no carbon compounds left to produce butter
unless the cow drew on stored bodily fats.

At that time all-year-round dairies had begun to
be approved and so the production of milk in the
winter months was a vital subject. " Pine boards
versus cornmeal " was being discussed, both from
a humanitarian and an economic standpoint. It
was then a common custom to allow the cows in
winter to roam in unprotected yards for the
greater part of the day and to go to some adjacent
stream for drinking water. The ice on the borders
of the creek and the steep incline of the bank often
compelled the cows to stand at an angle of thirty
degrees with the horizon while they drank ice-cold
water. I pointed out that this method of trying to
make ice cream direct from the cow was an uphill
business and had always proved a failure. I
recommended that the drinking water for the dairy
cattle not only should be brought into the stable
but that it should be warmed to blood temperature;
for we had discovered at the College by experimentation that a cow in full milk and in full feed
in winter would drink from fifty to seventy pounds
of hot water daily.

To my astonishment I found myself far in advance of my audience in these ideas. When this last statement was made the president of the association rose and remarked sarcastically that the University must have a "steam-boiler breed of cows." Then a leading dairyman jumped up and asked whether the professor had ever plowed! With such comments and questions they all but hissed me off the stage and utterly discredited my propositions.

In the evening the Association was elaborately fed in the basement of the Baptist Church. I went to the banquet a little late and finding the distinguished members all seated at the head of the table and not being invited to join them, I took a seat at the foot — apparently the proper place for a "hayseed" professor. When the speaking came on I was toasted in hot water in an elaborate and witty fashion. That night was one of the most miserable of my life as I sleeplessly tossed, wondering what would be the result of my being so completely "frozen out" by so important an organization.

I was much surprised therefore to receive an invitation to address them again the next year, but of course I accepted for these were the very people

I wanted to reach. I learned by this experience
not to get so far in advance of my hearers as to
wholly lose their sympathy; yet in the intervals
between sessions I still had to flock by myself.
Year after year I attended these meetings, winning
favor gradually until, after fourteen years, it happened that the meeting was again held in the same
place where I had first attended and the same president was in the chair. Before going to this convention I hunted up that first paper which had
been so ridiculed and brought it down to date.
That same old paper I read at the meeting as if it
were quite new and it was discussed in a friendly
and intelligent manner.

At the close of the discussion I disclosed the fact
that this was the same address that I had delivered
before them fourteen years before. I reminded
them jokingly of the chilling occurrences of that
meeting, remarking that they had made it so hot
for me then that it had taken all these years for
my temperature to become normal. The Honorable Harris Lewis, a man of great wit, was then
the leader in dairy matters; he was a man who appeared larger when seated than when standing and
when he arose deliberately everybody laughed, as
they usually did, anticipating a humorous remark.

This time, in his unique way and peculiar voice, he said: " Professor, you've got us — let us down easy!"

I served two terms myself as president of this association somewhat later. But this long story has been set down here for the purpose of showing how professors of agriculture were discounted in those early days by practical men. It was as hard to get a respectful hearing among the farmers as to get a foothold in the universities; and it required infinite patience, perseverance and good temper.

Since that time one of my former pupils, Professor H. H. Wing, has served two terms as president of this association; and at times many agricultural students have been employed throughout the State in testing herds of cows as to quantity and quality of product. Professor R. A. Pearson, also one of my former pupils, who succeeded Professor Wing in the dairy department at Cornell, became State Commissioner of Agriculture and took great interest in the development of the dairy cattle of the State. Mr. Pearson has now (1912) been elected to the Presidency of the Iowa State Agricultural College at Ames.

The dairy interest of New York which had altogether in 1900, 1,501,608 milch cows and 98-466 other cows, now constitutes a great industry and unquestionably, the work of the college of Agriculture has greatly promoted its development. There would certainly have been no such rapid growth nor friendly coöperation between the University and the dairymen, if I had nursed my personal grievance when the Dairy Association so coldly received me on my first appearance. It proves again that he who is right can afford to wait for recognition.

As the number of students increased and the University grew it became evident that the class in agriculture must be held to three terms of continuous work if their interest was to be maintained and the college to hold a creditable position. As there was no one to take my place I decided to forego my vacation, which by agreement I was to take in mid-winter, and for many years I taught for nine months and ran the farm in the summer, thus working three months longer than other professors for the same salary. But during the mid-winter term I felt at liberty to attend agricultural meetings at a distance and to travel somewhat to familiarize myself with farming conditions, whenever I could provide for my class. From 1880 onward I lectured five times a week throughout the year and spent two afternoons in each week with my class in the fields or shops or barns. Beside this I gave one lecture a week to the students in veterinary science and three lectures per week and some laboratory work to the winter course students. Besides all this instruction I gave attention daily all the year round to the management of the University Farm and after 1887 to the Experiment Station work, besides filling many speaking engagements in the Eastern States and in Canada.

Sometimes I would set an examination for the class on Friday which would relieve me of one day's teaching and with Saturday give me two free days; sometimes I took the entire class with me on tours of inspection. The railroads were liberal, either transporting us free or at a minimum rate of one cent a mile. At one time a party of twenty-two of us made a week's visit to Canada where we were royally entertained by the Government; twice the class of twenty-five students attended the horse show at Madison Square Garden in New York City; several times they visited the sugar factories in the State and, in later years, they were dismissed to attend in a body the three days' annual meeting of the Horticultural Society of Western New York; on many other occasions we made short visits to noted herds and farms.

The College was then so illy equipped with illustrative material that it was necessary to take students on such trips or they would have missed valuable opportunities; for a considerable part of an agricultural education consists in making comparisons, good and poor being only relative terms. I am quite sure I was the first professor to adopt this method of instruction but now it is common enough in varied forms.

My frequent absences from the college resulted in my being criticised for neglecting my classes —the critics not knowing of my vacation agreement. The fact is, things only went smoothly when it was understood that I was really doing two men's work, so I found it best to ask the President's permission if my absence was likely to extend beyond one day and later this became a rule for the government of all instructors. Once, when seeking permission from the President for a three days' absence, he remarked wisely that it was a good thing sometimes to give a class a rest so that they might catch their breath and become normal.

Before I came to Cornell the nursery firm of Ellwanger & Barry, of Rochester, New York, had offered to donate to the University a large assortment of plants for an arboretum. Since the campus was somewhat hilly and would need grading before plants could be set out and as no comprehensive plan had then been made for locating the college buildings, and, most important of all, since the University lacked funds even to pay its instructing staff properly, the offer had been politely declined. This firm was, naturally, not very friendly to Cornell afterwards, not having understood all these reasons.

There were other reasons as well why the horticulturists of the State were not enthusiastic about the College of Agriculture. Our Professor of Botany and Horticulture, an overworked man in delicate health, was unable to make the effort to heal this breach by attending the annual horticultural meetings — perhaps the most important convention of the State. Mr. Barry, so long as he lived, was the President of the State Horticultural Association, which was unfortunate from our point of view.

How to overcome this unfriendliness was a question to which I gave much thought. I myself was quite unknown to the agricultural leaders. I was looked down upon by the scientists, ridiculed by the farmers, on trial even at Cornell, and worst of all, I knew almost nothing about horticulture.

For two or three years I contented myself with taking a back seat at these meetings and with trying to make acquaintances at the headquarters' hotel. Finally, while making investigations in the preservation, loss and value of farm manures, I accumulated some good material for a talk and I knew that the orchardists were needing information about plant foods. So that year I went up to the meeting with my facts condensed and freshly in mind, if I could get the chance to present them.

Upon greeting Mr. Barry, I remarked that if there chanced to be a few unoccupied minutes I would like to make some brief remarks. That day and most of the next passed and I had come to the conclusion that the ice was yet too thick to be broken, when like a clap of thunder, in his stentorian voice, Mr. Barry called upon Professor Roberts. I had no time for stage fright — which to this day I am subject to — but rushed forward from the rear of the hall and without even my notes to guide me, I made the best short talk I had ever given. The subject I had chosen was pat and new and the facts were so convincing that they appealed to my audience. Then was made a big hole in the ice that never after froze over.

Next year I received a formal invitation to address the Association and I believe I was asked to speak at every subsequent meeting as long as I stayed at Cornell. Later Professor Comstock took a most useful and active part in these yearly deliberations and his work was supplemented and finally taken over by his assistant, that able economic entomologist, Professor Mark V. Slingerland, now deceased.

One of the best results of this victory over prejudice was that this society afterward came to the rescue — along with a number of other agricultural associations — when the College of Agriculture went to the Legislature and asked for an appropriation of $250,000 with which to erect buildings for its exclusive use. Some years previously the State had appropriated $50,000 for a dairy building, probably because Professor Wing and I had taken such an active interest in the dairy husbandry of the State. This building served its purpose until a larger and more modern one became necessary. It was then taken over by the University and made a wing of Goldwin Smith Hall. The sum of $40,000 was allowed for it, which, added to the $250,000 obtained from the Legislature, made a sum of $290,000 for the agricultural buildings and their equipment.

I am fully persuaded now that the most valuable

9

and productive work I did for Cornell was in advertising the work we were doing — making the college known among farmers and legislators through whom we secured not only buildings but support and sympathy in the promotion of more intelligent husbandry.

The old and honored Agricultural Society of the State for many years held its annual fair at Albany, Utica, Elmira, Rochester and Buffalo in a somewhat regular rotation. It was so expensive to provide suitable buildings at each of these cities in turn that they were never adequate and as a consequence there was a steady decline in attendance. For lack of interest on the part of exhibitors the affairs of the Society had fallen into the hands of a few life members who conducted the annual show to suit themselves and, it was believed by some, for their own profit. In order to save the Society, a few annual and life members joined in securing many proxies on the quiet and at a certain election of officers outvoted the old management and their following. The old ring died hard; the lock on the office door of the secretary — who had drawn a liberal salary for many years — had to be picked and removed and a complicated new one substituted for it before the newly-elected secretary could get or hold possession.

After much discussion the new administration decided to build a permanent home for the fair that the exhibitors might always find suitable protection for their exhibits. The city of Syracuse was selected as the most central for the permanent location. Naturally, the other cities became antagonistic and for the next few years the new management had all it could do to keep the fair going. Large State appropriations for the erection of buildings and for premiums were made annually; yet notwithstanding this, the Association would come out at the end of every year in debt. At this juncture the Board of Managers requested me to accept the nomination for the presidency, assuring me that they were certain I could be elected. They agreed that I was most favorably known throughout the State and had much influence with many state and county organizations; and they hoped that my non-partisan influence would do much to heal the old jealousies and re-unite the leading farm interests in this enterprise.

I was elected by an almost unanimous vote — the chief opponent from the old board not appearing at the election. Almost my first official act was to sign — with other members of the Board — a note at bank for something like thirty thousand dollars. The next season premiums were reduced, expenses cut and much hard work done and for once the Society came out even. I was again elected to the presidency but the weather being unpropitious that year at fair time, the usual deficit appeared. From this time on it was necessary to obtain large appropriations to keep the fair going; and as the legislators grew tired of these annual deficits it became necessary to elect as president some man who had great influence with the powers at Albany. And meanwhile the permanent debt steadily grew larger.

Some time before my retirement from Cornell the horsemen of the State became dominant in the Society and an honest effort appears to have been made to save it by repairing the old buildings, adding new ones, and by making trotting and other horse exhibitions the principal feature of the show. Well-known and wealthy men and some strong politicians took the management, fast horses became the chief attraction and increased appropriations were obtained from the Legislature. So far as I am able to learn the Society again became strong and useful, largely through the influence of Commissioner R. A. Pearson.

The most interesting part of my connection with the New York State Agricultural Society is still to be related.   The University Charter granted by the State provided among other things that the president of this Society should be an ex-officio member of the Board of Trustees of Cornell. When I became president of the Society my colleagues on the faculty congratulated me on having reached this distinguished position but the Executive Committee of the Board of Trustees had no words of felicitation for me.   The President of the University sent for me and quietly informed me that a professor could not be permitted to sit as a member of the Board or the Executive Committee and that the Board of Trustees could unseat me by resolution or they could ask for my resignation.

I replied that as to the first procedure, the Board was powerless to unseat me for the Charter of the University was above them; and that as to my resignation, it had always been before them. Some years earlier I had made it plain to President White that my resignation was always metaphorically in the hands of the Executive Committee.   I had never had any intention of taking part in the business of the Board of Trustees because matters often came up for consideration which were vital to the other professors; but I had supposed that as President of the State Agricultural Society I could come before the Executive Committee to urge the needs of my own department as an official equal and not on my knees as a suppliant for favors.

As it turned out I only went once before the Committee in my official position and that by appointment. At that time I explained the work of the College somewhat at length and my connection with it, showing them how many winter vacations I had given to the University without compensation.

The Acting President, Professor Crane, afterward said to me that I had made an excellent presentation of my case and that it had made a profound impression upon the Executive Committee. From that time on, at any rate, it appeared to me that my road was a little easier; it is certain that the Acting President became convinced then of the justice of my claim for a larger recognition of the College of Agriculture. I have reason to believe that he often helped it in a quiet way through his close connection with the Board and the President of the University. We became fast friends and on the anniversary of my seventy-first birthday he wrote me an appreciative and congratulatory letter.

When I met the President of the University on his return this matter of my being an ex-officio trustee came up again. What had hurt me most was that the trustees had not given me credit for having sense enough to know that it was not suitable for a professor in one college to take part in framing rules for the government of other colleges or to be present when other professors and teachers and their departments were being discussed. I said to him that the position of Trustee of Cornell University was the highest one I ever expected to reach; and that I was proud of it because I had won it fairly and not by any political pull. It was to me an indication that my work in the promotion of agricultural education and farm practice was appreciated by the people of the State at large; and neither he nor the Board need have been afraid that I would intrude.

TRAVELS AND AGRICULTURAL OBSERVATIONS

There was a lapse of sixty years between my first journey to New York City when I was a lad and my last one a few weeks before I came to California. But in that long time, though I have not been round the world, nor to Europe more than once, I have nevertheless travelled a good deal for a busy man of limited means. I have lectured at various times in twenty-three of the States and in three provinces of Canada; I have travelled in nearly every State of the Union for the specific purpose of becoming acquainted with American agriculture. With this object in view I have crossed the continent seven times, made six trips through the Southern States, and many shorter journeys throughout the New England and Middle States.

Even from the car window I could often tell whether the farmers of a given district were receiving an adequate return for their labor and it was not very difficult to surmise the principal causes of failure. The two factors which always stand out prominently when one is studying agriculture at large, are the productive power of the land and the exact knowledge of farming possessed by those who till it. If vast areas of land which now bring but a meagre return to those who till them were thrown out of cultivation and re-forested there would be great gain not only to the individual but to the community as well. An average yield of two-fifths of a bale of cotton per acre (200 pounds) cannot provide a fair living for those who raise it, much less a profit, when the infinite pains and severe labor required to raise cotton are taken into account. There is still good agricultural land in the cotton belt which might be cleared to take the place of that which should be re-forested.

In my last annual report to the Trustees of Cornell University I urged upon them the desirability of purchasing small areas of the depleted lands near the University and of re-clothing them with forests so that the people of the State and the students might have proper object lessons in reforestation; and that some of the lands which were running their owners into debt might not furnish inferior products, raised at a loss, to glut the markets. To cite a specific case: within twenty miles of the University and within a mile of a railway station there was a farm of 100 acres offered to me for $1,000. There was still enough timber in the wood lot to remind one of the valuable timber which had once covered these rolling acres but which had been wantonly burned or sawed into lumber and sold for six to eight dollars per thousand feet — scarcely more than the cost of marketing.

Such ideas as these were the result of my various journeys. If I were now starting out in life I would certainly choose forestry instead of agriculture as my profession. The one is constructive, the other destructive; the first husbands and protects the soil for future generations, the second has filched from our common mother her precious, long-stored treasures only to thrust her products upon an unresponsive market. All the people ultimately suffer when there is taken from the soil that which by the laws of economy is not wanted and which sells in the market for less than it costs to produce it.

I always had a peculiar love for the woods about my native home in central New York; and so when I was very tired I used to go, in later years, to that little corner of the University Farm where the oaks and pines, the chestnuts and hemlocks, were still standing in their pristine dignity; and lying flat on my back, admire their straight, limbless trunks, their graceful swaying, and their soft eternal worship of their Maker. I was therefore particularly pleased when once upon a time I was invited to deliver an address at the dedication of the Federal Experiment Station building at Orono, Maine. Here I thought I should behold not only the useful lumber pine of New York but lofty spires fit for the masts of great battleships and merchantmen. Imagine my disappointment when, soon after crossing the line into the State of Maine, I saw several saw mills cutting thin box-boards out of logs nearly all of which were smaller than telegraph poles. The railway station building in this pine-tree state was finished inside with *Georgia* pine!

"So withered stumps disgraced the sylvan scene
No longer fruitful and no longer green."

I frequently visited Simcoe, Canada, and at Tilsonberg, where there was a tedious wait for railway connection, I would wander off into the near-by clearings where infinite toil was being expended to destroy the beautiful trees, in order that sunlight might be let in to poor, water-soaked patches of land which by no possible means could ever be made to pay more than the meagerest reward for the labor of clearing and tilling them. In travelling from Montreal to Stambridge — a French district — we passed through long stretches of level country which had been cleared and fenced into little fields by the severest toil. So many and so high were the fences that from the car window the whole countryside looked like one vast, continuous rail pile; only small areas of cultivated land adjoining the railroad track could be seen;

all else was hidden by rails — nice, straight rails, neatly and carefully laid on other nice, straight rails, and these on others as high as the French farmers could reach. All this reminded me of the little fields of my boyhood and the interminable fences, and of myself, a discouraged, spindly lad mowing the weeds out of those "snaky" fence corners on muggy August days. I must declare that splitting such rails never produced a Lincoln but rather, poor white trash — Lincolns are born and they split rails only under protest!

Afterward I travelled in western North Carolina and there I found the farmers fencing in "moonshine" cornfields with black walnut rails — making barriers that were horse-high, bull-strong and pig-tight. In that country of narrow-chested pigs, the rails had to be split small and it was not uncommon to find old fences twelve and fourteen rails high, the practice being to lay new rails on top as the under ones settled, to make it horse-high.

During all my earlier travels I was securing lecture material by this study of things at first hand — things as widely scattered as were the homes of the students whom I taught — for at that time agricultural literature was very meagre and unreliable. These journeys gave me opportunity to observe the failures and successes along many lines of agriculture in widely separated districts and saved me from making many mistakes, while forming my judgment and improving my teaching capacity.

While travelling in South Carolina, on one occasion, I was the guest of a wealthy and intelligent planter who had somewhere earned the degree of M. D. I commented to him on the great value of the oil expressed from the cotton-seed — which had formerly been wasted — leaving all the nutritive value of the seed for feeding and fertilizing purposes and in an improved condition. To which he replied, quite seriously, that he never sold any cotton-seed because he considered the oil which it contained a valuable fertilizer — everybody knew how beneficial soapsuds were when used around fruit trees and the soap was made of oil and grease! This reminds me of another superstition that I picked up in the South. While visiting Mr. Joseph Jefferson, the well-known actor, at his cattle ranch and winter home near Vermillion Bay, Louisiana, he told me that he had cured his rheumatism by carrying a potato in his pants pocket until it had dried up into a hard little sphere; and to prove one part of the story he exhibited the potato!

At the time I first travelled through the Southern States it seemed to me that they were not yet ready to receive northern settlers into full fellowship and I did not, therefore, invest in land then; but in 1887, having occasion to go as far west as Wisconsin to deliver some lectures, I turned aside to visit the Agricultural College at Starkville, Mississippi, where my friend, Professor F. A. Gulley, was in charge of the agricultural department. We discussed the industrial future of the South and particularly land values and prices. He took me to see 1,400 acres of bottom timber land which could be purchased at a great bargain. The forest was largely of hickory — an indication of good soil — rather thinly scattered over the whole tract, a part of which was subject to a slight overflow in the spring, which could easily be drained. The price of the whole tract was one thousand dollars. The owner was not in town but when I had looked up the title and found it good, I tried to borrow money from my friend for a deposit to bind the bargain. But he said that as there had been but one sale of land in all this district since the War, it would be quite safe to let the matter rest until I got home. Meanwhile the agent of the railroad had suspected my business from the fact that I purchased a ticket from Chicago at a reduced rate as a "land-looker;" he followed me up, bought the land for a thousand dollars cash and before I got home sold it at an advance of about four thousand.

You can imagine my chagrin when I received this news; but Professor Gulley wrote me comfortingly, that there were plenty of just as good bargains almost anywhere in the State. In this he was mistaken, however, for this particular tract was rich, *virgin* soil while most of the other lands had been depleted by many crops of cotton. A few months later he wrote me that he had found 1,140 acres of level land without fences or buildings on it which had laid out to commons ever since the opposing armies had skirmished over it in 1863. As a matter of fact, my son afterwards ploughed up cannonballs in several places on it. It was situated about six miles from Canton, the County Seat, and three miles from a little railway station — Walkerton — and sixteen miles north of Jackson, the Capitol of the State.

Dr. James Law, Professor F. A. Gulley and myself formed "The Mississippi Land and Cattle Company, Limited" and bought the land at two dollars per acre, the owner receiving $1.50 and the agent $0.50. My son, Perry B. Roberts, (Cornell '87) was made manager of this plantation which was to be a cattle ranch. He at once constructed a large pool — and afterwards nine or ten more — by excavating earth-dams in the low draws, so that the ranch could never run short of water. This afforded a supply for the livestock in several places so that they did not suffer from thirst because of the long distance to water.

The attempt to make a good well near the buildings was unsuccessful because of the fine clay soil; so a large underground cistern was built which received rain water from the eaves of the buildings at the beginning of winter and which was sealed up before the warm weather came on in the spring. With this precaution the water remained cool and sweet all summer.

A simple house, a large barn, a small horse barn, two cabins and later, a silo, were built. The ranch was fenced into four fields of unequal size with a three barbed-wire fence of which the oak posts were made eight feet long so that when one end rotted off the staples could be cut and the posts turned end for end. The farm was supplied with brood-mares, for workstock largely, and with a herd of from one to two hundred cattle, bought from the owners of the abandoned open lowlands round about.

After getting well started the Company also rented 640 acres of land adjoining at 25 cents per acre; but soon after this the fence laws were so changed that the planters were compelled to fence in their livestock instead of fencing in their crops. This produced a shortage of young cattle in the country round and compelled the company to change its business radically. We had been handling from 800 to 1,000 cattle yearly, buying in lean cattle and selling as soon as the butchers would take them. The change in the law compelled us to give up the cattle business practically and to take up cotton raising.

About this time Professor Gulley sold his fifth interest to Professor Law and the land was then divided into five equal parts in value, I taking over two-fifths and Professor Law three-fifths which included the buildings. Meanwhile I had purchased 640 acres adjoining at $6.00 per acre upon which my son now built a small house and barn and several cabins for tenants. This gave the Robertses somewhat over one thousand acres, one-third of which was woodland, useful only for providing firewood.

The enterprise was never fully successful because the soil had been much depleted and the rotation was such, necessarily, that recovery crops could not be grown in a large way to restore the power of the land; and because of the compulsory change in the kind of agriculture pursued. In 1900 my son sold the whole place and moved to California.

TRAVEL IN EUROPE

I have often wondered why many educated travellers who have visited the Orient and the Art Centers of Europe have apparently not seen anything except beautiful cathedrals built by the toil of half-starved workmen, picture galleries and fine scenery. I suppose I must be too practical — too just to "the ox that treadeth out the corn" — to rave over these lovely things while human beings suffer. American travellers cannot but see the enforced and grinding thrift and the terrible effects of ages of drudgery upon the peasant classes. Look as I may, the dark background of these works of art and nature blur my vision and rob me of much of the pleasure that others seem to gain from them. I do not see the use of laboriously building spires that the unlettered throng may believe they reach in some mysterious way

the very throne of God. God dwelleth in the
hearts of men here and now and not on " the pin-
nacles of the Temple." Such thoughts as these led
me to study the land and the people chiefly during
my two months' stay in Europe rather than to visit
historic piles of brick and stone.

In the summer of 1878 it was at last my privi-
lege to study European agriculture at first hand.
With several Collegians I embarked on a slow
Dutch steamer and at the end of two weeks
landed in Rotterdam. I enjoyed my visit to the
great University of Leyden because it had been
built by great heroism and suffering; and to other
places of historic and educational interest; but
most of all I enjoyed a two weeks driving trip
through North Holland and Friesland in company
with Professor W. T. Hewitt who was then making a study of the Friesian dialect. These two
provinces are largely given over to the rearing and
exportation of cattle and to the dairy industry. I
was greatly interested in the herds of black and
white dairy cows, especially as I had an order to
make some purchases. This variety of cattle, now
known as Holstein-Friesian, has been bred nearly
pure for at least five hundred years on the polders
(reclaimed lakes) and hence has ripened into a

most prepotent breed. American dairymen have now become much interested in them and have imported many select specimens.

Early in this narrative I have related how I became interested in this breed and now I had the opportunity of inspecting not only their home but also many hundreds of the finest animals in the Netherlands. But good as the breed was, the American breeder has greatly improved it. I append the recent official performance of one of the most noted producers, "Pontiac Pleione No. 61102", owned by Stevens Brothers, Liverpool, New York:

"100.1 pounds milk in a day; 645.1 pounds milk, 26.1 pounds butter in seven days; 2,752 pounds milk, 103.57 pounds butter in 30 days. She dropped her calf in 11½ months after calving, and in the 365 days produced over 26,000 pounds of milk — an average of 71¼ pounds of milk and 2 pounds 10 ounces of butter per day. She has never been dry since she first freshened as a two-year-old and is one of the finest types of Holstein-Friesian cows living."

Since the above was written the three-year-old record has also been broken and it thus appears that my instincts, even way back in 1875, were right when I purchased the three Holsteins for the University Farm.

The dairy farmers of Holland are intelligent,

law-abiding and skilful. The men do not work as slavishly as do most American farmers, since little tillage is practised, the land being given over to hay and pasturage. Most of the land has been reclaimed from marsh, lake and sea, and is naturally moist and fertile; and, unlike the land in our own country, it retains and even increases its productive power. One must praise the skill and perseverance of these low-country farmers, but most of all I admired the contained, simple and intelligent life of both landowners and tenants whose acres have grown no less rich by use after hundreds of years.

The city of Haarlem interested me very much as it is the center of the culture of Hyacinths, Tulips, Auriculas and Carnations. Holland claims the merit of having promoted floriculture to a greater extent than any other country in the world. As early as 1836 and 1837 the flower trade of Holland assumed the form of a mania and many people speculated in bulbs to their great gain. It is recorded that a " Sempre Augustus " tulip bulb was sold for 13,000 florins — $5,220 — and an "Admiral Eukhuizen " for 5,000 florins—$2,000. A single Dutch town is said to have gained upwards of ten million florins by the sale of tulip bulbs alone in one year, and a speculator in Amsterdam realized 68,000 florins in four months from the sales of bulbs.

I found that the staid Dutchman had some characteristics in common with Americans. A Dutch farmer's boy brought out his school atlas that I might show him where I lived; think of my humiliation when I saw that the United States on his map was pictured somewhat smaller than the Netherlands! But our geographers treat some foreign countries in the same way. In the course of visiting various farms in order to purchase cattle, I was able to eat and chat with the residents and their families and to form some idea of their home life and habits. It is enough to say here that I formed a most favorable opinion of the Dutch people.

In England, the rural conditions were quite different. The landowner usually resided in some distant city or at his country home that was often far away. The renter, the country gentleman, usually resides on the land and operates largely through a bailiff, who stands for a non-working boss such as may be found on the ranches of wealthy Americans, though, in some cases, the landowner deals directly through the bailiff. Under the bailiff may come still another, the sub-boss,

who works with the laborers. Try as I would I
could not get to see the peasants at home in their
neat-looking little brick houses, nor could I get an
invitation to eat with them. A bailiff informed
me that the peasants would be so embarrassed that
they would not sit down at table with me even if
he took me into the houses.

The tillage crops and the livestock were usually
of the best, but the farm implements and the
methods of using them were often of the worst.
In a hayfield I saw a man leading a fine horse
which was hitched to a spring-toothed, self-dump-
ing hay-rake — why he walked I could not discover! Near by two women were rolling up the
windrows into bunches and two men were pitching
them onto a wagon which had wheels and rack so
high as to necessitate pitching the last of the load
more than ten feet up! There were two loaders,
two women raking the scatterings of the pitchers,
and a boy leading one big horse hitched to the
wagon. It must be said, however, that that load
of hay was as trim and square-cornered as a barn,
when it reached the rick.

I visited Laws and Gilbert's wonderful experiment farm and learned much as to methods of
experimentation from both of them. It was a

great treat to see with what broad intelligence, infinite patience and pains they carried on their work. It made me realize, as never before, what true investigational work meant. But the practical application of their work was not being appreciated in England nor did the farmers appear to be able to interpret the results in terms of their own activities.

I visited also the sewage farm and the agricultural college at Seiencester but neither of them gave me any valuable information. The sewage farm was so overstocked with weeds and filth that one could not admire it. If the farm had been of nearly pure sand instead of soil lacking porosity, the vast amount of sewage might have been disposed of without offense to the surrounding country.

The agricultural college of which I had heard my colleague, Dr. Caldwell, speak, was situated not far from the experiment farm of Dr. Laws where Professor Caldwell had studied for a time. The college was very disappointing for I had read and admired many works on English agriculture and where I had hoped to learn something of the best methods of British industry, I found, instead, an institution struck with dry rot.

In addition to the ten days given to the study of
English agriculture while driving through the best
agricultural districts and going from town to town
in the evenings by rail, I interviewed many country
gentlemen to gain a clearer idea of the rural life
of England. Two days in London enabled me to
take a second-story-bus ride down Cheapside,
visit Kew Gardens, the Parliament House and the
Bank; to ride the whole length of the two-penny
tube, to see Cleopatra's Needle, erected on the
banks of the Thames and to eat dinner at a swell
restaurant, just to see how our wealthy cousins
got away with so much American beef.

In France, I spent about one-half my time in the
country districts and since everybody knows about
beautiful Paris, I shall spare the reader a description of what I saw there. My objective point in
the country was the village of Nogent le Rotrou
in the province of Eure et Loire, the center of the
Percheron horse district. While selecting four
of the best specimens of this breed to take back
to America, I had opportunity to mingle freely
with the farmers and to observe their modes of
life and thought. The country round about was
not unlike Tompkins county, New York; the farms
were of fair size and the fields were fenced and

used for growing grass, for hay and pasture, wheat, oats and similar crops. But their leading and most profitable industry was the rearing of horses for the city market and for export. The work stock on nearly every farm consisted of brood mares which were used not only for tilling the land but for raising colts as well. These were usually sold when old enough to wean for from $100 to $200 apiece. Why the American farmer does not adopt this practice in a modified form during the winter months when the work stock is idle, is more than I can figure out, since we have good barns and often plenty of preserved, succulent forage in winter.

In the fall these French colts are sold, the fillies to one dealer and the colts to another who may keep them for from one to three years, when they are again sold to other dealers or to farmers for use on the light sandy land. They are often put to work at two years of age. Sometimes they are sold and resold several times while they are being fitted and pushed along towards their final destination. The lot of horses which I first inspected consisted of about twenty stallions which were being used occasionally to till the large farm and all of which were for sale. I may explain that in France

it is not customary to emasculate the males nor to
keep males and females on the same farm. It was
very confusing at first to see so many stallions of
several distinct types, for I did not know the exact
type of the breed that I wished to buy. At the
very first farm at which we stopped the farmer
tried to bribe my interpreter — an old acquaintance of mine who was then residing in France;
but finally, after much inspection of farms, much
horse-talk and bantering, for the Percheron horse-
man is a French Yankee, I bought four young
animals at a cost of $725 apiece.

Near the village where we were stopping there
was an old castle perched on a bluff, three sides
of which were rocky and precipitous. The old
moat — now waterless — draw-bridge and the
portcullis were all there; and the castle — dark,
damp and dingy — in charge of a keeper, made
one feel

"Like one who treads alone some banquet hall deserted
 Where lights are blown and guests have flown
 And all but me departed."

It reminded me through what sorrow, stress and
crime humanity had passed before it learned to
place any real value on love and justice. There
at the bottom of that moat lay the bones of many

a brave man, bent on robbery or reprisal, or perhaps on rude justice. I came away from it with a sad heart and I had no desire to visit another castle.

It appeared to me that the people of France whom I saw might be roughly divided into three types: first, the dwellers at Paris — small, dapper, polite, pleasure-loving; second, the peasants who live in small villages not far from the cities and till their little ribbony strips of land by manual labor, who were lacking in enterprise and intelligence; their lives being uneventful and circumscribed there was little opportunity to break loose or to do things in a large way — in short they appeared to be on a dead level. Third, those living on the larger farms remote from centers of population — particularly those engaged in the production of livestock — who were large of frame, virile, progressive and the reverse of dandified. These were more like the Friesians who boast that they were never in bondage to any man.

Just now much is being written about small farms and their economic value. When discussing this matter with a friend who is keeping a large stationery and sporting-goods store, and who employs seven clerks, I asked him what would be

the result if he should divide his business into eight
stores and place them under as many separate
owners. Without hesitation he answered: "We
would all live on half rations or fail." So it is in
farming: if for no other reason, economy of effort
forbids cutting the land into holdings the size of
those in the Isle of Jersey and of some portions of
France. This is the day of energy, other than
that contained in muscle and he who pits his mere
physical powers against horse, steam and electric-
ity must fall far behind and be content with little.
But small as well as large farms have their place
in a country so diversified in agricultural productions and wants as is America.

The South:

As I was bidding Mrs. Roberts goodby on leaving for my summer in Europe I remarked that I
supposed it was my duty to go to Europe but I
would much prefer to go to New Orleans. From
my boyhood this Southern city had taken a hold
on my imagination. When I was just a little lad
one night when stories were being related around
the fireside someone told this one:

"Once on a time a grocer purchased a barrel of
New Orleans molasses. After he had sold a part of it
the molasses ceased to run. Knowing that the barrel

was not yet empty he broke in the head and found the toe of a negro in the spigot hole! "

This seems to be a gruesome and silly story but it must be remembered that slavery was then constantly in mind and many stories of its brutality were current. I presume that many of them were untrue or exaggerated but how was I, a little country boy, to know that any more than that the stories of the boatmen on the Erie Canal were of the unsalted variety! Anyway, I wondered and wondered why they cut off the darkies' toes. After I went to bed I would picture the scene and no other foolish little story ever so aroused my imagination as this one. I determined when I should be grown up, to visit New Orleans and find out all about all these horrid practices. As the years went on and sectional strife increased, my desire grew until New Orleans was the one city in the whole world I most wanted to see.

A few years after my return from Europe when War and a clearer understanding of our national differences had tempered my judgment, I found myself on a bitter-cold February night in the eighties, in Chicago, aboard of a Pullman car headed for New Orleans. As I laid away my overshoes and top-coat I remarked to my wife that with them I put away my prejudices. I have never spent a more satisfactory day in my life than that first day in New Orleans, viewing the celebrated Mardi Gras. As no other of my youthful desires had held me more firmly, so no other gave me more satisfaction in the realization. While spending many hours at the great levees watching the army of roustabouts discharging and loading ships, I pondered much on the question what place the negroes could justly fill in an advancing civilization. What more I saw and learned about the negro problem will not interest you since I found no solution for its difficulties.

From New Orleans we went to the land of "Evangeline;" saw the ' Cadians and visited the great sugar plantations near the border of Lake Pontchartrain where the water ran away from the bayous and rivers instead of toward them. While inspecting a great cane-crushing machine my friend put his hand on the piston and remarked that it had cost him $10,000. He explained that one year in the midst of the cane harvest, the piston broke and the engine and a man to go with it were immediately placed on a steamer for New Orleans; it was ten days before it could be repaired and the machinery set going again and during that time a severe freeze came on and the cane which would have been worked but for this weather, was lost. This mill was usually run day and night and the quantity of cane which could be passed through it was almost beyond belief; and it and the six-mule team hitched to the largest plow I had then seen, made farming in the North seem quite in-significant.

It is impossible to describe fully the two widely different kinds of agriculture in the South. One is planned on a very large scale in districts which are most productive, the other is, to all intents and purposes, peasant farming, conducted on "patches" many of which are of irregular shape and size and often seamed and gullied by reason of the lack of grass roots and humus and by the peculiar physical condition of the land and heavy rainfall. Large areas of land appear so forlorn, so wrinkled with the creases of the plow and so tired with raising cotton, that they have lost all agricultural and sylvan charm. Some friends travelling in March, 1910, from New Orleans to San Francisco via the Southern Pacific, wrote me that after more than a thousand miles of such land they thought it merely useful to "hold the country together."

My visit to Petit Ance — Avery Island — Salt Island — had nothing to do with agriculture at the time but it did result in the introduction of the Holstein-Friesian cattle into that wet prairie country which is near the Gulf of Mexico. Salt Island had once been heavily wooded and was an island only at unusually high tide. It owed its name to a curious circumstance. The owner of the Island upon joining the Confederate Army left a boy of twelve at home in charge. When salt became very scarce the lad conceived the idea of boiling the water which trickled from the deer-lick or spring hole to get salt. At first a single sugar kettle was used, afterward, when it proved a success, several others were put in place and a considerable quantity of salt was obtained. The slightly salty water was thus soon exhausted and the father returning home just then, set workmen to digging a shallow well. When a depth of about twelve feet was reached they struck rock and Mr. Avery asking that a piece of the rock be thrown up to him, instinctively tasted it, to discover that it was pure rock salt! The surface dirt was then scraped away and the salt was mined in the crudest manner. Then General Butler, having heard of the mine, sent a gunboat into Vermillion Bay,

10

shelled the Island and held possession of it until the end of the Civil War.

When peace came, Mr. Avery contracted with a New York firm to open and work the mine. I had the pleasure of standing in that great underground, dome-like room which was about twenty feet high and more than forty feet in diameter, where salt, pure-white and glistening was beneath, above and on all sides. Large blocks and cubes of salt were being blasted from the sides and ceiling, so large that they had to be broken up before they could be lifted to the surface. There they were passed through a corn-mill and ground fine or coarse as desired. A railway has now been built from the main line to the salt-mine, a distance of about ten miles.

I am reminded by this of the other tales I have heard of the difficulty of procuring salt during war times. The father of one of my students who lived at Laurens, South Carolina — a man who had dug up the lead pipe which served to carry water from a hydraulic ram to his house and sent it to the army to be melted up into bullets — when they could no longer get salt, leached the earth in the smoke-house from which a small but very impure supply was obtained. When even this gave out the oldest boy drove a long distance to the seashore, boiled down sea water and brought back a small quantity of very bitter salt.

Petit Ance — Salt Island — bordered on good fishing grounds and as it was the only elevated timber land for many miles, it was the natural place for an Indian village. This brings to my mind an interesting legend connected with the Island. It seems that when white men first came to this region they asked the Indians who lived on it. The Indians replied, The Evil Spirit, and said that neither they nor the white men would go there. The legend which had come down to them was that once upon a time the Evil Spirit got angry, made a great noise and then killed all the people on the Island. This points, no doubt, to some volcanic disturbance in early times — which prevented the Indians from returning to live there.

When the shafts were being sunk for the salt mines there were found pieces of symmetrically woven basket work along with charcoal, ashes and many pieces of burned and rudely decorated earthenware. While I was there such pieces were being brought up from which I selected some pretty specimens. The owner of the Island be-lieved that many Indians must once have lived there who had been driven out by a cataclysm and that this had furnished the basis for the legend, and this theory was corroborated by the fact that the salt-rock stopped abruptly below as though it had been broken off from a deeper bed and thrust up as a "fault."

SECTION IV

CALIFORNIA AND THE WESTERING SUN

(1903)

CALIFORNIA AND THE WESTERING SUN*

In accordance with the rules of the Trustees of Cornell University, I retired in June, 1903, after almost thirty years of continuous service and with the honorary title of Professor Emeritus. After selling and dismantling the house on East Avenue, Campus, in which we had lived for twenty-four years, we went to Palo Alto, California — the seat of Stanford University — where my daughter and my elder son were living.

While Mrs. Roberts and our daughter went to Honolulu for a few months, I superintended the erection of a large two-story bungalow at 1148 Bryant street in this pleasant little College town. In this commodious dwelling Mrs. Roberts and I spent eleven years; and owing to the neighborliness of several professors who had been Cornell students and the nearness of our three children and their families, we were able to adjust ourselves happily to this radical change of environment.

Until I was finally established in Palo Alto I had not fully realized how much I needed rest

---

* Refers chiefly to northern and central California.

after so many years of strenuous activity. During the whole fifty years of manhood I had taken scarcely more than a few months vacation altogether. I might perhaps have continued some line of agriculture in California after I had had a good rest, but I determined at that time to devote the remainder of my life to light, healthful outdoor work in order to keep physically fit; and in lending a helpful hand to those who had not been so fortunate as I had been.

For I have been exceptionally fortunate both in my family life with the one woman of my choice and with the three children whom we lovingly reared together and who remained to gladden our declining years. And no less happy in the profession which chose me so early in life and which has always seemed to me the finest in the world and the only one for which I was by nature fitted.

By old-fashioned thrift Mrs. Roberts and I had accumulated a little capital at the time we went to Cornell in 1874. My salary was then $2,200 which was gradually raised to $3,000 per year. As time went on I received another $500 as Director of the Federal Experiment Station; $500 from the State appropriation for the promotion of Agricultural Science and had perquisites

incident to my position which were probably worth
$500 more.   Thus during the later years I was re-
ceiving the equivalent of $4,500 per year.   The
cost of living was much less than now-a-days; our
habits of life were simple and, in spite of the fact
that we gave our children every educational advantage, we always saved something as we went
along.   By judicious investments, mostly in first
mortgages on small properties at moderate interest, I have amassed in the course of my life
about $60,000, all of which I have now given to
my children.   After I left Cornell the Carnegie
Foundation gave me a pension of $1,700 a year.
It is now the joke among them that " Father cannot spend his income " for I find my pension more
than enough for my needs and am again accumu-
lating a little in the bank.

I was more fortunate than many present-day
professors, in receiving a fair salary quite early in
life and still more so to be among the first American teachers to have my services recognized by a
substantial pension.   I cannot help observing that
if all young professors and their wives were as
careful as we were, they might also launch their
children modestly in spite of the increased cost of
living and the generally higher standard in this
modern day.

In the summer of 1905 my son Roger and I
built for investment three cottages in the village
of Sunnyvale, nine miles southeast of Palo Alto,
doing practically all the work ourselves except the
plastering, plumbing and wiring. This work I
greatly enjoyed. The drive of forty-five minutes
morning and evening behind a good roadster and
the seven hours carpentering, gave me a new lease
on life. What joy in eating and sleeping when one
has done a good day's work!

Although I was getting rested my general health
was not very good and after nearly a year's treatment by my family physician I went in 1907 to
Lane Hospital in San Francisco for a capital operation. In about six weeks I was able to return
home but it was more than a year before I was
able to walk with ease and meanwhile I had to
have plates to support the arches of my feet which
had broken down because of my weakness. This
operation cost me $750 and with the additional
charges for nursing and hospital care the total
bill amounted to about $1,400. I am tempted to
digress to comment on the situation of a poor man
under similar circumstances.

Although I had many opportunities to observe
agriculture on the Pacific Coast during my first

years here I did not take much interest in my life-long occupation until after I recovered my health. I did return, however, to Cornell in 1905 and 1906 to deliver short courses of lectures; and also gave two short courses at the Polytechnic School at San Luis Obispo, California. Later, in 1912 and 1913, while my son Roger was Manager of the University Farm at Davis I gave short courses there; and during the winter and spring I gave one parlor lecture a week to six mature men, teachers in High Schools, who wished to prepare themselves for teaching agriculture in secondary schools. Four of the six were made principals of schools the next year and they were kind enough to say they thought their course with me had helped them to this promotion. This summer (1915) I read a paper on " The Trend of Agricultural Practise," before the Association for the Promotion of Agricultural Science at their annual meeting which was held in connection with the Panama-Pacific Exposition Congresses at Berkeley. At this meeting there were about forty of my former colleagues and students, all of whom are engaged in some line of Agricultural Science; and it made me feel that I am indeed, what people have sometimes called me — " The Father of Agricultural Science."

I have been asked many times " What do you think of California ? " And I have to answer that it is in many ways the most wonderful State in the Union. The unending variety of soil, climate, aspect and people, makes it difficult, indeed impossible, to give an adequate description of this land which borders the sinuous shore of the Pacific for nearly 2,000 miles. It contains more than 157,000 square miles and as to heat and cold, all the climates of the habitable world. In a few places for many successive days Honest Old Fahrenheit may record from 100 to 125 degrees but you don't have to stay there for you can motor, if you like, a hundred miles or so, enjoying the scenery, and land in a snowbank a century old. On the way back from your joyride you may select a ranch anywhere between these two extremes. Yes, you may select your climate and your farm — anywhere from 10 to 10,000 acres — whereon to expend your enthusiasm, your brains, your brawn — and your ducats.

You can choose land where you would be compelled to grow the " Kids " by moral suasion for there would be no beech or birch within a hundred miles; or you may take to the timber country and dwell comfortably in a hollow redwood tree. If you are a little uppish and decline to live in the basement of a tree-house 300 feet high, you may choose a knoll " with a view," in the abruptly roll-ing forest lands from which you may cut 50,000 feet of merchantable " Oregon Pine " per acre. Or you may locate by the river bank and till the rich alluvial bottomland; and provided you have a safe retreat above the melted snow which comes down in the spring, you may have without charge a glorious water-view perhaps ten to twenty miles in breadth.

Then there is the " Hog-wallow" land which costs less than the river bottoms, upon which you can spend from twenty to twenty-five dollars in levelling so that it can be flooded for the cultiva-tion of rice which is becoming common in the in-land valleys of the State.

And this reminds me of the Legend of Hog-wallowland. Once in prehistoric times there was a genus of swine with noses so long that they could stand on one side of a river — provided it was not too wide — and root up the sweet flag in the soft marsh on the other side. In size they were between a rhinoceros and an elephant; and belonged to the one-toed pachyderms, being cov-ered with bristles about the length and size of a lead pencil. When they became violently enraged they could erect their long, stiff sharp spikes and thus protect themselves from their smaller and more active enemies. These swine did not live in the marshes but on dry land but when it rained they wallowed freely and in this way, it is said, the hog-wallow land was given its present uneven contour.

Did you ever see any hog-wallow land? Well, if you had you would have given it a bad name. However, if not too much impregnated with alkali it may be made, when levelled, to yield prolific crops of rice. The semi-rock hardpan near the surface conserves the waters of irrigation; and, if holes are blasted, there are many varieties of orchard trees which will thrive on the plant food which lies below the hardpan.

I will describe but one more kind of California soil which the Native Sons tell me can be plowed and tilled with perfect satisfaction for only about ten days in the year. This soil is called "Adobe." That's Spanish for unburned brick; and when you want to turn your farm into a brickyard all you have to do is to plow the land when it is wet, shape the brick, let them lie in the sun awhile, and build your house.

Between this heavy adobe and the drifting sands of the semi-arid districts there are many varieties of soil which if suitably tilled and artificially supplied with moisture when necessary, may be made to produce enormous crops. These large yields, often four or five times the average, are not uncommon in the better districts, but the new comer should base his expectations on the even keel of the average for a series of years.

One of the peculiarities of California soil is the extreme variations which often occur within a few rods — variations due to prehistoric geologic causes into which I need not go here. The descriptions given above may be a little ironical and perhaps not scientific but the landseeker will be likely to get clearer ideas from them than from the latest geological disquisition. In any case it is intended to warn him that on the Pacific Coast he would better inquire and listen and wait before purchasing land; and then wait awhile longer and secure some more facts before buying farm lands at the very high prices now asked for them.

Anyone familiar with eastern agriculture and the farming of the Middle West finds a sharp contrast in some of the practises which prevail in California. If you chance to drop off at any thriving village or "city"—as many modest towns are called out here — you will discover that every second man you meet owns a "ranch." In a few minutes' conversation you will discover also that his holding consists of only two, five, ten or at most twenty acres and that it is for sale or for trade, for cash or other equities. When I first came to California it seemed to me that everybody's place was for sale; which is merely to say that the Californian is adventurous and ready always to move on to something new.

If his ranch is bare land he prices it at $150 to $200 per acre; if set to trees or vines at $300 to $350; if there is a habitable house, a shack of a stable and a well, the price will run from $350 to $450; and if the plantings are in full bearing and all the necessary appliances are on hand for irrigating, tilling, harvesting and marketing the crop, the price will be $600 to $1,000 per acre. This figure may include several hundred or perhaps a thousand trays, boxes and the like, for everything — even the work stock, cows and chickens — goes with the land. As our forbears would have said: "All the hereditaments thereunto belonging." When a Californian sells out he takes only his household goods with him.

PROFESSOR ROBERTS ON HIS SEVENTY-FIFTH BIRTHDAY

At his son's ranch, Yuba City, Cal.

To illustrate the high values of small ranches I may give a few specific instances. Only the other day when I wanted to sell a small house and lot in town I telephoned to my friend the Professor who owns a fruit ranch in the Santa Clara Valley and asked if he could not trade my place for such property. I expected to give something to boot — for ten acres is enough even for me now — but back came his answer instantly: "Oh no, Professor! That Santa Clara land is too high-priced — $600 per acre at least. Why, I've been offered $500 per acre for my own ranch of 80 acres, sixty of it in prunes, cherries, peaches, olives and English walnuts, some of which are not yet in bearing!" Incidentally I may remark that many professors and school teachers in this country, and some ministers own such home places.

A few years ago my son and I were interested in producing seedless raisins in Sutter County. The first year raisins were sold for five cents per pound and the gross receipts from them was $3,000; the second year the price was nine cents and gross receipts $4,000; the third year, at six cents per pound the gross receipts were $3,550. About one-half of the receipts goes for labor *et cetera* and the other half for the use of the land

and equipment. This forty acres (30 in vines) was sold for $9,000. Some of the neighbors did better than this and some not so well — I judge that this was a fair average.

Farming in California comes the nearest to gambling of anything I have yet tried and even at that it is better than gold mining. Professor B——— asked a California ranchman if raising cherries was profitable. "Well," replied the rancher, "I made one crop which paid me the full value of the orchard and I have never kept any accounts since." And yet while travelling through this same district I have observed that most of the cherry trees had the "die-back" and were scarcely better than soil-robbers. There are a few restricted areas where cherries do well and when they do well, they do very, very well; but when the district is not adapted to them they do nothing at all. What is true of cherries is measurably true of most other fruits, especially of apples. This again illustrates the extreme variableness of the soils in this country.

The Santa Clara Valley, agriculturally speaking, is about fifty miles long and ten miles wide, and is the home of the prune. Prunes are sold by an established standard, eighty to the pound being the base. Just now they are selling at the packing houses for $100 per ton; 70s would sell for $110 and 60s for $120 per ton; while 90s would be worth $90, 100s $80 per ton and 101s $79 per ton. That is, the price rises or falls $1 per ton for each point. At the packing houses they are washed, softened, packed and shipped East in carload lots. The jobber, the railroad, the wholesaler and the retailer take their toll of the price and the consumer ultimately pays three times as much as the producer receives. The only way for the consumer to reduce this price is to come to the Santa Clara Valley and eat prunes off the trees for they retail here in California at a price only slightly lower than in Chicago. Prunes from other districts bring a half a cent less per pound as a rule. The yield per acre of dried prunes varies widely but ignoring the extremes, it may be put down at one to one and three-quarters tons per acre for which the ranchers are now receiving five cents per pound. A good bearing orchard with buildings and equipment has recently sold for $600 per acre.

The two great farming valleys of the State — there are hundreds of smaller ones — are the Sacramento and the San Joaquin (pronounced San Wah-keen). The head waters of the Sacramento

are found at snow-capped Mount Shasta, 325 miles
away and it receives the tumultuous waters of
several smaller rivers which take their rise in the
higher Sierras.   All these rivers coming down
from the north and northeast furnish abundant
water — in springtime often too abundant — and
have played an important part in soil formation.
They still play a great part in crop production and
in some places have to be restrained by levees.
Much of this diking has been made necessary
by extensive hydraulic and dredger mining on the
upper reaches of the rivers which tend to fill the
riverbeds with slickings.   When the dikes break
and the river overflows the slickings may be deposited on farmlands and do great damage even
to the extent of throwing the land wholly out of
cultivation.

Formerly grain raising was the almost universal
occupation of the ranchers but now orchards, vineyards and alfalfa largely occupy the land once devoted to wheat production.   In 1900 twenty-eight
and a half millions of bushels of wheat were raised
in California but in 1913 the production was only
a little over 4,000,000.   Most of the cereals are
raised without irrigation and barley is still raised
in large quantities.   In 1913 over 33,000,000

bushels were produced much of which, crushed, was fed to domestic animals. Very little is used within the State for malting but more than seventeen and a half million bushels were exported. The average price at the farm last December was sixty-eight cents per bushel.

As a rule the grain-raiser does not till his land nearly so well as the fruit-raiser. This is partly due to the fact that not so much income can be secured from grain and not so much capital has to be invested to raise it; and partly because orchards and vineyards may be intro-tilled throughout the growing season. I have never seen better tillage than most of the orchards and vineyards receive in California. No rain falls during the period of surface tillage and therefore every weed may be destroyed and a fine earth-mulch maintained by which moisture is conserved up to the time of harvest.

The acreage devoted to alfalfa is rapidly increasing. Three to five mowings may be secured each season with an average yield of a ton per acre to each cutting. Milch cows and dairying are also rapidly increasing and it may be hoped that the alfalfa and the cows will stop the excessive soil depletion which is the result of the grain-raising of the past thirty years. It is important that this great valley of the Sacramento — an area as large as the State of New York — should be saved from further soil depletion and its productive value maintained that the children and grandchildren of California may have as fair an opportunity as their forbears had.

The Sacramento Valley has more rainfall, a darker-colored and more uniform soil than the San Joaquin Valley and its soil retains moisture well. Both valleys are well suited to the production of beans especially the smaller varieties and that too, without irrigation. Beans are the most staple crop that can be used to form a rotation and can be planted in May and will grow all summer without irrigation. In 1913 over three million bushels edible beans were produced, but Michigan still leads with a production of more than four million six hundred thousand. Between 1900 and 1910 New York increased its bean product by 23 per cent, Michigan by 192 per cent and California by 405 per cent — in another decade California will doubtless be ahead.

Rice was introduced into the United States in 1647 by Sir William Berkeley and into California a half a century ago; but until six years ago it was

not produced in quantities sufficient to indicate that
it might become a profitable crop.   There are in
California large bodies of land, adobe and alkali
and those where the hardpan is near the surface,
which are not well adapted to the crops now
raised upon them but upon which rice may be
grown very profitably.   In 1914, 16,000 acres
produced 8,528 tons which were sold at an average
price of forty dollars per ton.

Last year California shipped out of the State
45,000 cars of oranges, each carrying about 400
boxes, and produced 65,000 carloads of raisins of
all kinds.   Then there are the almonds, and English walnuts and olives and melons besides.
And that reminds me of a story which aptly
illustrates the abundance of melons in some
localities.   A ranchman had a big crop and
the price did not warrant him in hauling it
to market.   There was an Indian Reservation not
far away on the edge of the Desert and it is well
known that Indians are very fond of melons.   The
farmer let it be known that any Indian could have
all the melons he could haul up a little hill just
outside the house gate, for two dollars, but if the
wagon stalled the price would be three dollars.
Soon there was a procession of wagons coming to

the ranch. But Indian ponies are not draft horses and generally the Indians would load on more melons than the ponies could pull up the hill. Then ensued laughter and shouts, pushing and whipping of horses until they took off a portion of the load. It was a great festival for the Indians and a countryside joke among the ranchmen — but the farmer made a profit even at two dollars a load.

Land values in the Sacramento Valley are not quite so high as in the Santa Clara and San Joaquin Valleys. The San Joaquin is the hottest of the three in summer and Santa Clara the coolest, hence the latter is the most desirable as a residential district besides being much nearer to the City by the Golden Gate. The San Joaquin is the home of the vine and wine and the seedless raisins; of melons and beans and peaches; of table grapes and a score of other edibles which are sent East throughout the summer and fall by train loads in double sections. We sometimes wonder at the fruit appetites of our remote eastern relatives.

The San Joaquin river and its tributaries take their rise in the Sierras, run northwesterly and finally mingle their waters with those of the Sacramento in Suisun Bay, a broad, shallow sheet of water bordered by marshes which produce quantities of tulis (bullrushes) and pasturage for cattle. Vast numbers of ducks and geese frequent the bay and marshes in spring and fall. Suisun Bay is some fifty miles long and empties through Carquinez Straits into the Bay of San Francisco which is itself sixty-five miles long and twelve wide at its widest, and through which these waters reach the Golden Gate and the Pacific Ocean. At the Carquinez Straits there plies the largest ferryboat in the world — so they say — capable of transporting whole trains of overland passengers at a single trip. These immense land-locked waters, which the Coast Range shuts in everywhere except at the Golden Gate — have much influence on the climate and upon the plants of the districts bordering upon them. In fact it may be said that the bay region has several climates and a flora all its own.

But if I began on this region also, this tale would never have an end. California is three times the size of New York, you must remember, with enough left over to cover Servia. The County of San Bernardino alone is larger than that little Kingdom over which twelve European States are now so fiercely warring. You see how hard a task I set myself in attempting to give you even the crudest outline of so big and varied a country.

But the ink in my pen still flows and my agricultural hobby-horse is not yet tired so I will go on to say that in the wide Valley of the San Joaquin it has become necessary to employ a land expert to assist the farmer and the colonist. Both the State University and the railways employ them to determine for the land-owners such difficult problems as how to provide, transport and conserve the water supply; whether to bring the supply from the mountains or to pump from the subsoil to the surface. Where the lift is from twenty to forty feet the problem is simple; but where the lift is one hundred to one hundred and fifty feet it is both more complex and more expensive. In large districts, although there may be no rain for six to eight months in the year, a full supply of water for irrigation may generally be reached within pumpable distance of the surface, and in a few localities artesian water is found.

The agricultural expert should not only be able to give reliable information as to water supply but also as to the character of the land, especially the subsoil. This can often be determined by the kinds of plants growing on the land but the character of the subsoil is usually determined by the use of a two-inch auger with an extension handle. In many districts a hardpan of rock or semi-rock or impervious clay is found from a few inches to a few feet beneath the surface.

The vast and undeveloped resources of so big a State cannot be discovered from the window of a Pullman or a tourist car. The railway line often runs through the worthless districts; and there are many secrets and more treasure in the sage-brush plains and mountain canyons than the stranger dreams of. Unfortunately, as soon as you settle in a promising region you discover that what you have to purchase is dear and what you have to sell is cheap. It often happens that what you want and what you have to exchange are far asunder. The *grainstack and the smokestack should be in sight of each other* if you are to dodge the numerous railway charges and the middleman. But when the best is done that can be done, still the distances, even within the State itself, are so great that both the consumer and the producer are at a disadvantage as compared with Eastern conditions.

From my window here in Berkeley looking out over the Golden Gate and across to Mount Tamalpais, the country seems small in this clear air; but when I read the invitation lying on my desk to attend a wedding in San Diego I begin to calculate the distances from one end of the State to the other. From here to Fresno, my other home, is 201 miles and it is 392 miles farther to Los Angeles; thence southward still another 127 miles to San Diego. If you wish to go to the end of the State it is ten miles farther to Tia Juana on the Mexican border where all wise persons purchase a return ticket. In fact it costs something like thirty dollars to go from one end of this State to the other — and wheat is only ninety cents a bushel!

The California climate is just like the soil in one respect — it is seldom uniform at two points even a few miles apart; so I shall pass this extensive topic leaving it in its ever-ready freshness as a suitable start for general conversation. Every Californian will tell you about its virtues and about his " view." Everybody talks about his view and thinks himself entitled to own one. Wherever you travel throughout the State the dwellers will show you the curves of the ocean beaches or the wide plains of arable land or desert waiting only for water; girt with foothills and far blue mountains beyond.

As to hills, lofty hills with lovely views, there is one in California for every family in the United

States and enough left over to satisfy all the real estate promoters. At this moment I see in the near distance the little mountainette "Tamalpais." If you climb it you think it is a knee-tester but if you ascend by the "crookedest railroad in the world" you get more thrills out of this double-up-and-turn-around track and the double-headed dinky engine than you do out of the view at the top.

Many of these mountains in California are richly stored with precious and mechanically useful metals but the forces of Nature have hidden them so cunningly that it usually takes two dollars worth of labor to discover one dollar's worth of metal. Now and then you may stumble on a rich "pocket" and then the cash flows to the mint; but you may have to be grub-staked a good many times before you strike it rich.

In attempting to describe the population of California I meet the same difficulty that I have already noted: there are so many kinds of people that it is all but impossible to give a clear picture which the stranger may comprehend and identify. However, everybody comes to California or is going to come, so I need only mention the classes that strike me as being different from those familiar to me in the East. California is a land

of contrasts — drifting snows and torrid deserts;
fertile plains and lofty mountains; noble rivers and
giant trees; precious metals, oil and wine; fruits
and flowers — and climates! If I could only dispose of its cosmopolitan people in ten lines like
that — but I can't!

There are still the Gold Seekers as in '49,
though the tourist will not see them for they dwell
alone in the high rocky fastnesses and by the
tumbling streams that roar through the mountain
canyons. The prospector is a silent man, living on
a "grub-stake" and on hope and faith. Nor is
the cowboy tribe extinct though you may not discover him in all his pristine picturesqueness except
on the farthest cattle ranges. He is slow to let
down the bars and bid you "light" but once you
gain his confidence all he has is yours. The cattle
business is not what it used to be, they will tell you,
as they recount the good old times when they ruled
the range. Uncle Sam, since taking control of the
vast grazing areas within the National Forests,
has tamed these rough and ready pioneers. The
number of range cattle is likely to increase and of
sheep to decrease because sheep injure the young
trees and grass whenever the pasturage is short
or the land overstocked.

A third class of people not found as a distinctive group in other states, are the real estate dealers. In all except the larger towns they are more numerous than the saloons; and both are likely to cause the traveller to drop his money. When you come across the Sierras you are likely to lay aside your conservatism, put some of your traditions on ice and become a joyrider and an optimist. I am told this is due to the climate. For this I cannot vouch but I do know there is a big pile of money dropped in unwise ventures out here.

The prospector, the cowboy and the real estate man are three picturesque types not to be overlooked but when I attempt to analyze the remainder of the population I am reminded of the answer a man gave when asked as to the breed of his dog. "Well, sir, he's one-half pointer and a quarter setter and an eighth spaniel and the rest just plain dog!" In California that fraction of the population which is just plain dog is pretty mixed but happily there are a goodly number of thoroughbreds as well that bay true. I have never known so many true men and women to give their training, time, means and enthusiastic labors to the cause of bettering civilization as I have met here. One looks on in amazement at the patience, courage and self-sacrificing spirit of this small minority of the people. My daughter puts it: "Majorities rule but Minorities lead the world;" and I would add that when the majority overtakes the minority, it will still be in the lead.

I am persuaded that this happy condition is due largely to exceptional freedom of thought and expression not only in general society but among the instructing bodies of the two great Universities. In no other public institutions that I have known are the workers accorded such latitude of speech; even the students are permitted to speak "right out in meeting." Autocrats, big and little, may muzzle the Press for political, financial and personal reasons but as long as the higher institutions of learning are free, civilization will go forward.

The leading newspapers of this State, I regret to say, are very generally muzzled. You have no more than subscribed for one than you wish you had subscribed for the other because none of them give you the facts. Not only are men and measures grossly misrepresented by paid correspondents who must obey their Masters' orders, but the editorials are often unfair and misleading and sometimes positively untruthful. There are perhaps only three newspapers of influence which may be relied upon, of which *The Fresno Republican* is the most conspicuous. The Editor is not only an able man but takes pains to get the facts and then analyzes them fairly and honestly. *The Sacramento Bee,* which has the distinction of furnishing the best news service, is also a paper of integrity though not so influential editorially.

How so many newspapers manage to live and find material with which to fill their columns is a mystery in a State only half a century old and so sparsely populated. But Californians are great readers of current publications and almost as much so of more serious ones, if I may judge from the recent demand in the Church which I attend for $465 for printing and papers for the coming year.

The Church, or The Churches (as you like) and other organizations for social betterment are too numerous to mention. Every denomination that I had ever heard of and many others are represented in California. The thoughtless reformer often asks why not unite them all, or at least the principal ones, and thereby save time, effort and expense. Well, that has been tried several times in the past and always failed; for in order to carry out the one-sect or one-church plan they were compelled to torture and murder vast numbers of good people of other beliefs. Even the Apostles wanted to try their hand at the one-church business: they reported to Jesus that some people were teaching Christianity but were not "following after US;" and Christ answered: "They that are for us cannot be against us."

One cannot long observe Nature's modes of action — which are God's — before discovering that dissimilarity is the supreme rule and that homogeneity is the exception. Nature is ever developing new genii, families, breeds, sub-breeds and varieties without end. The vegetable and lower-animal kingdoms thrive in groups innumerable and fulfill the purposes for which they were created; so why should mankind with infinitely higher functions and nobler aims be confined to one race or one color, one form of government or a single church?

We are happily becoming free — Truth is making us so — and no longer must diverse races and beliefs be coerced into narrow traditional grooves. I am glad there are so many varieties of churches and of vegetables for now I can select those which will best promote my spiritual and my physical development. There are not even yet enough

THREE DEANS IN 1914

I. P. Roberts, Dean of College of Agriculture, Cornell, 1874–1903; L. H. Bailey, Prof. of Horticulture (1888–1903) and Dean, 1903–1912; T. F. Hunt, Prof. of Agronomy, Cornell, 1903–1912, and Dean at Univ. of California, 1912 ff.

churches and sub-organizations within them to furnish congenial opportunity for the millions of earnest men and women who desire to make the world better. All we need is that these varieties shall live harmoniously together.

A little weekly journal lies before me and I quote from its pages: "Assorted Conventions and Congresses to the number of 115 are scheduled for the last two months of the Panama Pacific International Exposition at San Francisco, from October fourth to December fourth." And I note further on that more than fifty livestock and poultry societies will convene at the Exposition in the latter half of this month, although we who have had the pleasure of entertaining our out of town friends had supposed that the Neap Tide of Exposition Conventions would occur when the schools opened.

Somebody says a new organization is born every minute but I have not heard of one for Professors Emeritus yet; and I am delighted if it be so, because with a few exceptions every organization which I call to mind is striving to accomplish some good work. Some of them, particularly the churches, deal with the problems of life as a whole. A glance backward into history reveals the fact that nations have flourished and maintained themselves just in proportion as they have practised the fundamental principles of righteousness with faith in the real man — the invisible man — who dwells within and governs the visible, clay-made man.

Five great problems were left by the Master for us to work out and fundamental principles were laid down by which they might be solved. The first is Religious Liberty. If the present be compared with the not distant past it will be seen that this is nearly attained and will soon be completely solved by its own momentum. The second, Civil Liberty, has made long strides toward the final end when men and women shall have full expression under laws made by themselves. It is just seven hundred years since twenty-four brave English Barons demanded and secured a share in the government of their Kingdom. It has been a long, hard struggle for the degree of liberty now possessed in our own country where twenty-four million Americans have the right to vote and a share in making the laws under which they live. From the Red School House on the four corners to the White House where the Head Master dwells the problem of individual liberty is well-nigh solved.

A late part of this greater problem is the Liberation of Woman from her social and servile bondage. For weary ages women have been the slaves

and mistresses of men.   If there were too many
female babies born they were slain like female
dogs and cats.   But only yesterday an election was
held in this State to vote on several constitutional
amendments and two referendums and the women
not only voted but two of the election officers were
women citizens — college graduates — who did
all of the responsible work while two old-time
political "hackneys" shared the wage.   All this
was within sight of the towers of the State University which has six thousand students, two-fifths
of whom are women.   From now on the problem
of feminine liberty may be trusted to the women
themselves.

How much the State gains by this accession of
a more conscientious if not more intelligent body
of voters can scarcely be reckoned.   In the four
years since women have had the ballot there have
been developed a large number of strong wise
women leaders and they are already making a
profound impression upon the State.

The fourth great problem, National Sobriety, is
now on the way to solution.   A nation cannot continue to exist unless it lives soberly.   Spirituous
beverages are in their ultimate effects depressants.
They steal the brains and scotch the balance-wheel
and then the human machine runs wild.   All our

lives we put brakes on our words and actions in order to become refined; but alcohol makes us unstable and away the fool in us goes without brake or balance, revealing the secret man in blasphemy, vile wit and brutal instincts. It is up to us of the Twentieth Century to put down the drink habit which has cursed the world so long and thus put a quietus on the long train of deviltries which have followed it. Now that " the better half " of the people are getting their rights or approaching them, I have faith that this one of the two hardest problems will soon find a nation-wide solution; for no woman wants a drunken or a drinking husband and no lady likes a man's feet under her table who stands on his rights and forgets his duties.

The latest, if not the last, of the great problems which we of this generation must face is War. All the hideousness and ruin of wholesale murder has been revealed. Our consciences have been enlightened and what was once bravery, patriotism, powder-religion, as well as what was good cheer and wine smartness, have become heinous sins. Sobriety and peace are twin brothers. We may ignore the light and sear our consciences and when opposed fight back. " Whom the gods destroy they first make mad." We are in the midst of

. such a world madness the end of which we cannot
see. Here too we shall have the help of the wives
and sisters upon whom the greatest burdens and
suffering of war and of drunkenness fall. We cannot be a peaceful nation without being a sober
nation; we cannot be both without going a long
way on the road of righteousness. The weak
things of the earth shall yet confound the mighty
and the purposes of God be accomplished in our
land. One shall not say to another — Knowest
thou the Lord — for all shall know Him even
from the least unto the greatest.

As I draw near to the end of my story and the
description of the land in which I have been an
onlooker rather than an active force, I am profoundly impressed with the changes and the improvements which have been made in the twelve
years since I came to reside in California. The
great seaport of San Francisco when I arrived was
half foreign and altogether provincial. Afterward it was a city rocked by earthquakes and then
a city in ashes. For a brief time it became a sober
city wherein were no saloons; and what a contrast
to its earlier, riotous self it was during that brief
period! Struggling in the midst of economic problems and industrial confusion it shortly became a

city ruled by bosses and looted by a band of thieves. Since then the uprising of the better stratum of the people has begun and now San Francisco is a restored city, far richer and more substantial than before its great disaster, and ruled with some degree of economy and honesty.

During all these bright and glorious months of 1915 the Golden Gate has been open to welcome all the Nations of the earth and has become thereby at last cosmopolitan. I have certainly lived to see astounding things. The mutual slaughter of nations is not new but the devastation of twelve European nations by machinery, is as wonderful as it is horrible. In my lifetime I have seen six Expositions beginning with Paris in 1878, but none compared in beauty or extent with the Panama-Pacific International Exposition. And the greatest wonder of all is the Panama Canal. None of these things impress me because they are big. Bigness is like millions, incomprehensible. Tall buildings may be made taller by the addition of a few more courses of brick or stone; tunnels and canals may be made longer by a few more blasts of dynamite; but the whole enterprise of building the Panama Canal is an eighth wonder which I am glad I have lived to see.

The Ancient Wonders were built by slave labor and the brutal sacrifice of innumerable human beings; this Modern Wonder has taught mankind how to preserve the workers in a tropical, miasmic climate and is therefore reckoned one of the greatest scientific achievements of the age. What the effect of the Great War, the Great Exposition and the Great Waterway will be upon agriculture throughout the world, it is impossible for me to conjecture.

And still the ink flows freely from my pen but rather than weary you I leave it to your imagination to complete this life of a farm boy. I have left much unsaid for my life has touched many that are still living and there are some things too personally sacred to be put in print; but otherwise I have written with the frankness of youth and with cordial goodwill. Before you have finished these pages I hope you will have become my friend and so I invite you to come and see me in this my adopted country. Come in the heavenly springtime but " bring your heavy wraps for while the days may be bright and warm the evenings will be cool." This is the stock advice of an acclimated Californian.

Bring your purse along too, for this country has

not yet shrunken to reasonable dimensions. Come with an open mind and leave your magnifying glass at home; for I would not have you searching for faults and fly specks. Rather bring your field glass and we will go to one of the thousand hills and take in all the vast stretches of fruitful fields and landscape beauty. Come quickly before I get old and dull and you shall receive the old Spanish settlers' greetings: "All that we have is yours!"

> From Earth's wide circling bounds,
> From ocean's farthest shore,
> Come memories ever sweet
> Of friends I've met of yore.
> Life still flows smoothly on,
> The days all pleasant run,
> As through the Golden Gate
> I watch the Westering Sun.

DEDICATION

And now to whom shall I dedicate this book?

I might dedicate it to my children but they know full well that long ago I dedicated myself to them. I would like to dedicate it to Professor Liberty Hyde Bailey, my colleague and successor in office at Cornell, but I fear his generous nature would not be pleased to be singled out from other true and faithful friends. So why not dedicate this simple narrative of a Farm Boy's life to the

multitude of friends who are scattered all along
the way from Canada to Florida, from Maine to
California?

To that host of Sunday School children of long
ago; to those mischievous boys and girls who received from me guidance and instruction in the
three R's — and sometimes discipline as well; to
that inspiring and almost endless procession of
college students who, class by class, looked up at
me from their seats with eager minds for thirty
years; and to that larger host whom I met at institutes and agricultural gatherings, and last and
most cordially remembered of all, to my college
associates and generous co-workers.

To this great multitude — the friendly harvest
of a long life — I dedicate this my last book, begun in the autumn of my days and finished at the
age of eighty-two. May it give as much pleasure
and inspiration to the reader as I have found in
recalling the friendships and activities of half a
century. May my life history be in some measure
an encouragement to aspiring farm boys wherever
they may be in their lonely fields!

   ISAAC PHILLIPS ROBERTS,
     AT DWIGHT WAY END, BERKE-
     LEY; OR FRESNO; OR PALO ALTO;
     CALIFORNIA.